Wonders of Speech

Wonders of Speech

Alvin and Virginia Silverstein

Illustrated by Gordon Tomei

Morrow Junior Books   New York

For Brandi Green

Library of Congress Cataloging-in-Publication Data
Silverstein, Alvin.
Wonders of speech.

Bibliography: p.
Includes index.
Summary: Discusses the many aspects of speech as
a communication device, including the physiology of
speech, how children learn to talk, how to speak
effectively, speech for the deaf, and talking machines.
1. Oral communication—Juvenile literature.
2. Speech—Juvenile literature. [1. Oral communication.
2. Communication. 3. Speech] I. Silverstein,
Virginia B. II. Title.
P95.S553 1988   001.54'2   87-31370
ISBN 0-688-06534-1

Contents

1 _Speaking of Speech . . ._

An attack of laryngitis can quickly convince you of how important speech is in your daily life—and how much you take it for granted. You start to say something, but no sound comes out of your throat. "What?" people say. "Speak up; I can't hear you." You try harder, and perhaps you manage to force out a few squeaks, but nothing that anyone can understand. Helplessly you point to your throat, and then you try other ways of getting your meaning across. Simple gestures work fairly well for some messages: For example, you may pretend to be tipping a glass into your mouth if you want a drink of water. But gestures leave plenty of room for misunderstanding, and some helpful person may bring you a glass of milk instead. You may have to carry around a note pad and pencil to write out your messages.

Trying to communicate without spoken words may seem like fun at first—like living a game of charades. But the novelty soon wears off, and you realize how laborious it is to have to play guessing games with gestures or write out complicated messages whenever you want something. How frustrating it is not to be able to answer people's questions or to make a comment when something interesting or funny or upsetting happens. When you can't speak, you realize how effortless talking normally is.

Visiting a foreign country whose language you don't know can give you a different kind of insight into speech. You can make sounds and form them into what seems to you to be perfectly meaningful statements. But the people you talk to don't understand you. And when they speak to you, their words are a meaningless blur of sounds. If you try very hard, you may be able to pick out a few words that sound familiar and figure out what they mean. You can get clues from people's expressions, from their gestures, and from their tone of voice. (You don't have to understand the language to decide whether someone is sympathetic or angry, for example.) But you can't sit down and have an enjoyable conversation, exploring each other's ideas and experiences. Communicating by speech is a two-part process, involving both a speaker and a listener. The speaker forms thoughts into spoken words that the listener can hear and understand. But the process doesn't work unless they speak the same language.

Communication is an active process on both ends. It is easy to understand how speaking is active. The speaker's mouth moves constantly, shaping and modifying the sounds that come out. Less obvious but just as important a part of this speaking process is the mental activity that goes on: first, selecting ideas to communicate, searching among

Speaking and listening.

the memory's store of words—the vocabulary—to find just the right ones to convey the thoughts, and assembling the words into an appropriate order to make them meaningful to someone else; then, coordinating the complicated sequence of movements of the breathing muscles, tongue, jaw, and lips necessary to shape sounds into words. You might think that the listener has a much easier job, just sitting there taking it all in. But good listening is an active process, too. The listener must first hear the words accurately, distinguishing among similar sound combinations like *bit* and *pit* (which may be pronounced in varying ways by different people). Then the listener's brain must sort out the meaning in the words. That involves not only searching the brain's memory banks for a list of possible

definitions of each word, but also determining their rela-
tionship to the other words in the sentence and consid-
ering the circumstances. A sportscaster at a baseball game
saying, "It's a hit!" will mean something quite different
from the reviewer of a new play uttering the same words.
In addition to evaluating the spoken words, the listener
must evaluate the nonverbal cues that go with them—the
"body language" that ranges from smiles and frowns to
hand gestures and more subtle variations of body position and tension.

There is plenty of room for error in the communication
process, error that can lead to misunderstandings. You
have to choose your words very carefully to "mean what
you say," and even then your listener may find a quite
different meaning. Your personal vocabulary is a collec-
tion of words that has been built up gradually all through
your lifetime from things that you have heard and read.
Your own interests and activities have helped to shape
the selection of words that you have learned, remember,
and use actively. No two people have had exactly the same
set of experiences, and thus no two people have exactly
the same vocabulary. Your listener may be unfamiliar with
some of the words that you use; or he or she may have a
somewhat different set of meanings for words that you
share. That's something to remember the next time you
find yourself arguing with a friend who perversely took
the "wrong" meaning from a statement you thought was
perfectly clear.

The Sperry Corporation has sponsored a study of com-

munication failures, which are a major cause of wasted
time, inefficiency, and frustrated plans in business. According to the Sperry study, the average person spends a
great deal of time communicating with others, either
through speech or through written or printed words. The
findings indicate that the largest fraction of a person's
communication time—about 45 percent—is spent in listening. This important activity is the first one a child learns
(the latest studies indicate that the developing baby begins to listen actively even before birth), but it is the one
in which we receive the least amount of formal instruc-
tion. About 30 percent of a person's communication time
is spent in speaking, which is the second communication
skill that a child learns—also without much formal in-
struction. The training in school is centered more on the
last two communication skills that we acquire—reading,
which takes up about 16 percent of the average person's
communication time, and writing, which averages out to
only 9 percent.

Communication can occur on various levels. First of
all, it can be *intrapersonal,* involving just one person
without any interaction with anyone else. You might
wonder how that can happen. A speaker, after all, implies
a listener, with a transfer of ideas or information from
one person to another. But whenever you *think* in words,
you are engaging in intrapersonal communication. You
choose words and put them together in logical order, just
as you would if you were going to speak them aloud. In
fact, you may sometimes find yourself running through

imaginary conversations in your head, trying out approaches for an important conversation with someone in the future or mentally replaying a past conversation and thinking of all the wonderfully witty and forceful comments you could have made. These mental rehearsals may help you to express yourself more effectively later, when you are talking with others. In some cases, when you are scheduled to give a speech or act in a play, you can take the rehearsing one step further and actually say the words out loud, practicing and modifying your pronunciation, tone of voice, and phrasing to make sure they will help to get your meaning across.

A large fraction of our time is spent in *interpersonal communication,* exchanges of spoken words between two or more people. In an effective conversation, the participants take turns being speaker and listener. The listener should be just as active as the speaker, taking in the words, finding their meanings, comparing the ideas and information received to past knowledge and experience, and thinking of questions that will keep the exchange flowing. Even though this kind of communication is a social activity, it also includes many bits of intrapersonal communication, too. As you listen, you think about what the speaker is saying, mentally work out your own replies, and perhaps try to anticipate what effect the replies might have on the other person. Nobody really "talks without thinking," but you can get yourself into some embarrassing situations or heated arguments if you don't do enough mental preparation before you open your mouth.

intrapersonal   interpersonal

mass communication

Types of communication can be distinguished according to who is talking and who is listening.

Another level of speech, *mass communication,* has become much more important in our lives than it was in our ancestors'. When you listen to a teacher's lecture in a classroom, hear a ball game on the radio, or watch a program on television, you are participating in a form of mass communication. In the past, people's exposure to mass communication came mainly through traveling storytellers or town meetings, and an individual speaker could reach an audience of perhaps a few dozen at a time. But now, through electronic technology, you can watch a play or listen to a speech knowing that millions of others are sharing the same listening experience with you at that moment, and still more may later hear the same words in replays. Satellite relays broadcast the news and other forms of mass communication all over the world. Thus, people from the most varied cultures and backgrounds now have a great pool of shared knowledge. Today, information travels around the world far faster than it traveled from one town to the next just a few centuries ago.

Speech communication can serve a number of purposes. A young child learns amazingly quickly to use speech to satisfy his or her basic needs for food and comfort. As we grow older, much of our speech is still involved with satisfying needs, although those needs grow more sophisticated and subtle. Try to count up how many times in the past twenty-four hours you have asked someone for something. Your communications may have ranged from simple requests like, "More mashed potatoes, please," to a complicated speech aimed at persuading people to vote for you in the school election. As a listener, you may have had to hear and evaluate a number of other requests and persuasions, from your mother asking you to clean up your room to the ads on television exhorting you to buy certain products.

Another important function of speech communication is to provide information. It has been estimated that people learn about 85 percent of what they know by listening. When you think about learning in this way, you probably think of "educational" situations, like a classroom lesson or a documentary film on television. But people also learn a great deal from casual conversation and even from programs on radio or television that seem designed purely for entertainment.

One of the most common and important uses of speech is for pleasure. We humans are talking creatures, almost from the beginning of our lives. A baby is vocalizing and babbling, experimenting with new ways of making sounds and putting them together, even before he or she has learned to sit up. Gradually the child learns how useful speech can be but still retains a sense of fun in various kinds of wordplay, gleefully experimenting with simple rhymes and puns. As adults we still enjoy the rhythm and rhyme of poetry, get a lift of the spirits from the pungent humor of a good joke, and gain deep satisfaction from a long talk with a friend. Speech is one of the most important ways we have of getting to know others and sharing ideas, thoughts, experiences, and emotions.

2 _How We Talk_

Take a deep breath, and then let it out slowly. Now do the same thing again, but this time make a conscious effort to make a sound, first while you are inhaling and then while you are exhaling. You have just been testing out a key part of your speaking apparatus, the structures that generate sound.

Our ability to make sounds is actually a by-product of another very important body function: breathing. Breathing provides a continual supply of oxygen, which is needed to release the chemical energy locked up in food materials. Without oxygen, the chemical reactions in the body would soon come to a halt; a person who stops breathing for just a few minutes may die!

The breathing organs look something like an upside-down tree. Air is normally drawn in through the nose and passes down a long tube that is like the trunk of the tree. The upper part of this breathing passage is called the _pharynx_. It is a double-duty passageway, shared by the breathing and the eating systems. The mouth cavity has an opening into the pharynx, and the lower part of the pharynx leads into both the *trachea,* an air pipe with heavy, muscular walls, and the *esophagus,* a food pipe that leads to the stomach. The trachea passes down through the neck into the chest, where it branches into the *bronchi,* two slightly narrower muscular air tubes. The bronchi in turn branch and branch again, into smaller and smaller tubes, each of which ends in a tiny air sac. The two masses of tubes and air sacs make up the *lungs.* The force for breathing is provided by two sets of muscles: a heavy dome-shaped sheet of muscle called the *diaphragm,* which forms the floor of the chest cavity, and the straplike muscles of the ribs and chest.

At the top of the trachea, where it joins the pharynx, there is a tough, muscular structure shaped like a triangular box. This is the *larynx*. It is made up of nine separate cartilages (*cartilage* is a tough, gristly substance, such as that which forms the framework of the ears) held together by muscles and cordlike ligaments. It has an opening in the form of a triangular slit, and two fleshy folds inside the larynx can come together like valves to close off the airway or open to allow air to flow freely through it. As part of the breathing system, the larynx serves to close off the trachea when the chest muscles contract in a strong exertion—for example, if you are lifting a heavy box. It acts as a lid, keeping the air in the lungs.

The human larynx also has another name—and another job. It is called the *voice box,* and it is the sound-making organ. The two fleshy folds of tissue that can close

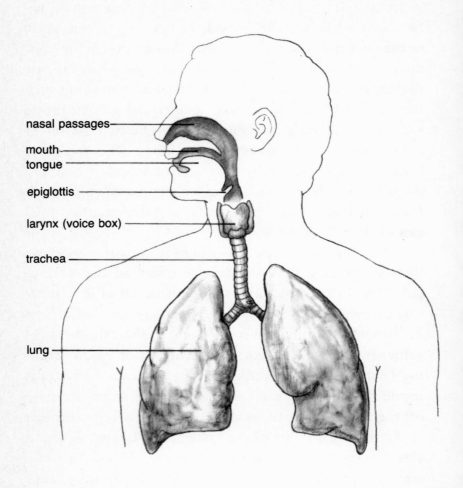

nasal passages
mouth
tongue
epiglottis
larynx (voice box)
trachea
lung

The human respiratory system doubles as a speech-producing system.

off the larynx are called *vocal cords*. When they are stretched tight they vibrate, producing sound waves in the flow of air passing through the larynx.

If you run your fingers along the front of your neck, you can feel the outline of the muscular tube traveling downward, and you may be able to make out the bulge of the larynx. (In adult men, the larynx may form a no- ticeable bulge, called the *Adam's apple.*) Now, placing your thumb and forefinger against the sides of the larynx, try the breathing exercise again. First breathe in and out normally, through your nose, without making a sound. In quiet breathing, you will not feel any vibration in the larynx. Then try saying "Ahhhhh" while you are breath- ing out. Now you will feel a distinct vibration coming from the voice box.

The vocal cords are not very well named. You might

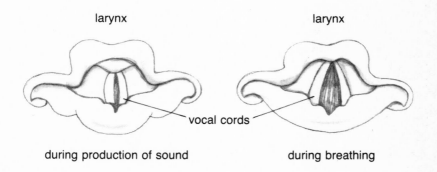

larynx   larynx

vocal cords

during production of sound   during breathing

The tightened vocal cords vibrate to produce sounds.

expect from their name that they would look like strings, rather than fleshy folds. Actually, they were named before people knew much about anatomy. They were called *cords* because they vibrate to produce sounds, much like the strings of a musical instrument.

The vocal cords do in fact work very much like the strings of a musical instrument. If you play the guitar, you know that when you tighten a string, plucking it produces a higher tone. The term *pitch* refers to how high or low a sound is. The pitch of a sound is determined by the *frequency* of the sound waves—how many waves are passing each second. (Each passing wave is referred to as a *cycle*.) The human ear can hear sounds from about 20 cycles per second (cps)—very low tones—up to about 20,000 cps—very high tones. The human voice can produce sounds in only part of that range. Middle C, for example, is 256 cps, and high C (two octaves higher) is 1,024 cps. Increasing the pull of the laryngeal muscles on the vocal cords tightens them and raises the pitch of the sound they produce. The lower and upper limits of a voice are determined by the size and structure of the larynx. A child has a small voice box, and a child's short vocal cords produce high-pitched tones. As the child grows, so does the larynx, and the voice becomes deeper. In boys, the larynx has a sudden growth spurt during puberty, with the result that the boy's voice changes abruptly from a childish treble to a lower, more masculine tone. (The adolescent boy's voice may "break" occasionally, producing an unexpected squeak, because he is still learning to use his new, larger larynx.) Irritation of the vocal cords can lower the pitch of the voice. That is why your voice gets lower when you have a cold. Smoking cigarettes or drinking alcohol on a regular basis can also lead to a lower-pitched voice.

In general, a man's speaking voice has its main tones at around 120 cps, while a woman's voice is higher, around 220 cps. Actually, however, the situation is somewhat more complicated. In addition to the loudest tone (called the *fundamental tone*), the voice also produces a series of progressively higher (and softer) tones, called *harmonics*. It is the combination of the fundamental tone and the harmonics that creates the distinctive quality of a voice and helps us to tell one voice from another even when they are speaking in a similar range of tones.

In singing, a person's voice goes up and down in pitch, following the melody. There is a kind of melody to speech, too. The pitch of the voice may vary with each word or syllable, and so may the loudness of the sound. These variations help to emphasize some words and downplay others, to point up questions or exclamations, or to signal the end of a thought. A person whose speech is mostly on a single pitch, a *monotone,* makes a very boring impression.

Like music, speech has a kind of rhythm, with periodic pauses acting as signposts to help the listener follow the flow of thought. Usually these pauses also provide opportunities for a quick intake of breath. Although it is possible to make sounds either when inhaling or when exhaling, we do our speaking while exhaling. People normally breathe in a regular rhythm, at an average rate of about fifteen breaths per minute, with each breath divided about evenly between the in and out parts of the cycle. When we speak, we change this rhythm, inhaling quickly and then letting the breath out slowly as we talk, until a pause in the flow of words provides an opportunity for another quick inhalation. (If you try to produce sounds or intelligible speech while inhaling, you will find it is possible but difficult; you probably won't be able to keep it up for long.)

The average speaking rate is about 150 words per minute. We tend to speak more quickly when we are excited and more slowly when we are being very serious. Generally, an inhalation provides the breath for a certain time of speaking rather than for a particular number of words. When we talk fast, we space our breaths over longer strings of words but still break them at logical places in the flow of thought. If we hesitate to grope for a word, on the other hand, we tend to hold our breath, saving it up so that it will last until the next appropriate breathing point. Fast-talking actor John Moschitta, who does radio and television commercials emphasizing the fast pace of modern life, has been clocked at an astonishing 534 words in 58 seconds. If you have heard any of his ads, you may have noticed that he takes huge gasping breaths to fuel himself for the long strings of rapid-fire syllables.

In addition to determining the pitch of the voice, the larynx regulates its loudness by varying the size of the puffs of air that come from the vocal cords. Muscles in the larynx adjust the air flow, with a more forceful flow producing a louder sound. (That is why your throat may feel sore after you have been shouting—your laryngeal muscles are tired and strained.) Variations of loudness serve to accent certain words and syllables. In the word *loudness*, for example, the first syllable is considerably louder than the second. We also adjust our voices automatically to compensate for competing noises, like traffic on a busy street or other conversations going on in the same room. At a party, people tend to talk progressively louder, vainly trying to "hear themselves think" over the noise of other people who are doing the same thing.

The larynx alone does not produce the sounds of speech. The vibrations generated by the vocal cords resonate in the tubular cavity of the pharynx. Resonance in the nose and sinuses may also contribute to voice tones. Nasal resonance is essential for producing certain sounds, such as *-ng*. But some people put too much nasal resonance into all of their speech tones, and the resulting sound makes an unpleasant impression. When you have a cold and your nose and sinuses are blocked, the lack of nasal resonance makes certain speech sounds indistinct.

Some of the resonating sound waves also travel up two narrow passages, the *eustachian tubes,* that connect the pharynx with the ears. You thus have a personal pipeline for listening to your own voice in addition to the sounds that you hear emerging from your mouth. Have you ever heard your own voice recorded on a tape recorder and

exclaimed, "I don't sound like that!" Part of the difference may be due to the quality of the tape recorder, which
may not faithfully reproduce all of the voice tones and
harmonics. But another important factor is that the voice
you hear when you speak is the result of both the sounds
delivered through your eustachian tubes and those that
travel through the air. Thus, you hear a highly personal
version of your own voice that cannot be heard by anyone else.

As the sounds generated by the larynx travel out through
the mouth, they may be modified by movements of the
tongue, lips, and jaws. Vowel sounds are made with the
mouth open. Changes in the shape of the opening deter-

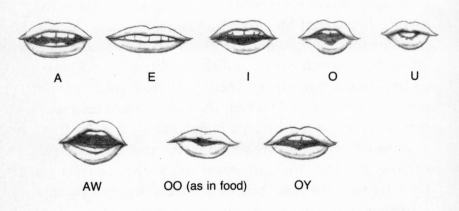

Mouth shaping different sounds.

mine whether the sound comes out as *ah, ee, ay, oo, oh, aw,* or one of the other vowel sounds. Interruptions of the air flow at one or more places in the channel from larynx to lips produce consonants. In some cases, the air flow is cut off completely, producing a momentary buildup of air pressure and then an explosive sound when the air is released. Examples of this kind of consonant are *p, t,* and *k*. The *p* sound is produced by closing the lips, *t* by placing the tip of the tongue against the gums behind the upper teeth, and *k* by placing the back of the tongue up against the roof of the mouth. Some other consonants are formed by narrowing the air passage without quite closing it, producing a hissing sound: for example, *f, th* (as in *thin*), *s,* and *sh*. The consonants we have mentioned so far are all of a variety called *voiceless consonants*. They are produced by modifying the flow of air without any vibrations being generated by the vocal cords—the sound-producing function of the larynx is momentarily turned off. Generally, each voiceless consonant has a corresponding voiced consonant, which is formed in the same way except that the vocal cords are vibrating. In English we have the pairs: *p* and *b, t* and *d, k* and *g, f* and *v, th (thin)* and *th (this), s* and *z,* and *sh* and *zh* (usually spelled in some other way, for example, the *zh* sound in *television*). You can feel the difference for yourself by placing your thumb and forefinger against your larynx and forming first a hissing *s* sound (no vibration) and then a buzzing *z* sound (vibration).

Ventriloquists master the technique of speaking with-

out moving their lips. It might seem that certain consonants, such as *p, b,* or *v,* could not be articulated clearly
without moving one's lips. But the ventriloquist uses some
clever substitutions to approximate their sounds—for example, a *th* instead of a *b* sound in the phrase "Boston
baked beans" can fool the listener into hearing the correct pronunciation. Typically, ventriloquists keep their teeth
closed to hide their tongue movements. Misdirection produces the illusion of "throwing" the voice: The attention
of the audience is attracted by the mouth movements of
the dummy, and so they "hear" the voice coming from
there instead of from the ventriloquist, whose lips are still.

Forming the whole variety of vowel and consonant
sounds—in quick succession, in the proper order, and fast
enough to provide for normal speech (some twenty to thirty
sounds per second)—requires a lot of nimble maneuver-
ing of the tongue, lips, and jaws. Each muscle contraction
must be carefully coordinated with the others, planning
ahead so that the sounds of the chosen words mesh
smoothly and glide into one another. This amazing jug-
gling act, which we perform so automatically that we are
not even aware of the effort, is controlled and coordinated by a number of specialized centers in the brain. It
is there that some of the most important work of speaking and listening occurs.

3 Mind Games: Speaking and Listening

Have you ever discovered, while in the midst of talking, that you couldn't remember a word or a person's name? You pause, groping for it, but your mind refuses to fill in the blank. "It's on the tip of my tongue," you protest. It's not really, of course, although this common phrase reflects the importance of the tongue in speech. The missing word is hidden somewhere in the filing system of your memory. It's not gone forever; most likely it will pop into your mind as soon as you relax and stop looking for it. It has just become temporarily unavailable because you haven't hit on the right cross-referencing key to find it.

Scientists don't yet know the full story of how memory works, but the basic outline has been built up. According to the current theories, memories are stored in the brain in chains of *neurons* (long, threadlike nerve cells) linked together in complicated sequences. When a neuron in the chain of a memory trace is stimulated—perhaps by something heard or seen or just a stray thought—it sparks a tiny flow of electric current, which is transmitted along the network by electrochemical reactions. The huge numbers of neurons in the brain (billions of them) and their many complicated interconnections permit memories to be stored with many cross-references. Suppose that you are talking about the James Bond movies and suddenly find yourself unable to recall the name of "the other actor who plays James Bond, you know, tall, lighter hair. . . ." While you are talking, your brain has embarked on a hunt for the name, first tracking down the clues that you have supplied and checking through its files of British actors, recognizable faces, and so forth. "I think his name starts with an *R*," you might muse as you zero in, or, "His last name has one syllable." Finally, you hit the right trigger to unlock the memory files, and you exclaim triumphantly, "Roger Moore, that's the one I meant."

An educated adult can recognize tens of thousands of different words. This is the *passive vocabulary,* words that one has heard or read and knows at least an approximate meaning for. The *active vocabulary,* on the other hand, is much smaller: The average adult uses only a few thousand words in everyday speech. This limited vocabulary is still sufficient to express an infinite number of ideas: The five hundred most commonly used words have a combined total of about fourteen thousand dictionary definitions!

The task of storing so many words and keeping them straight is simplified a bit because the brain breaks them down into components. One type of breakdown is into convenient units of meaning, which language experts refer to as *morphemes.* Some morphemes are the roots of words, such as *good, come,* or *trust.* Others are prefixes or suffixes that can be attached to the roots to add or change their meaning. The prefix *un-,* for example, introduces a negative connotation or changes a word's meaning to its opposite; the suffix *-ness* changes an adjective to a noun. In the word *untrustworthiness,* four morphemes are strung together, with *un-, -worthy,* and *-ness* successively modifying the meaning of the root, *trust.*

Another type of word breakdown is into units of sound, called *phonemes*—the various vowels and consonants. Using this kind of analysis, the brain can readily recognize words that are heard and distinguish among them, even if they are unfamiliar; when a person speaks, the brain puts together strings of phonemes to form recognizable words. The phonemes form a sort of alphabet for the ear, but it is a longer alphabet than the twenty-six-letter one we use for written English. To keep all the sounds distinct, for example, we need a way to differentiate among the various ways of pronouncing *a* in words such as *bat, ball, father,* and *state.* We need a symbol for the *th* sound in *thin* and another for the *th* in *this.* A list of English phonemes would also have to include a symbol to describe the *zh* sound in *azure* and *vision.* All together, there are about forty phonemes in spoken English, with about twenty of them vowel sounds. Other languages have phonemes for sounds that do not occur in English, such as the rolled *r* in Spanish, the guttural *ch* in German, and the *u* in French (which is actually an *ee* sound, pronounced with the mouth pursed up for an *oo*). Some English phonemes don't occur in certain other languages. An Italian, for example, has trouble distinguishing between the English words *win* and *wing,* because the *-ng* sound does not occur by itself as a phoneme in Italian.

The task of identifying phonemes is complicated by the fact that people have their own individual ways of pronouncing them. Variations of speech from one person to another are just as great as variations of handwriting, and in addition to these individual differences there are also distinctions that characterize people from different regions. A native of Boston, for example, might pronounce the name of the famous New England college as *HAA-vid,* someone from the South might call it *HAH-vid,* and a person from a middle Atlantic state would articulate both *r*s distinctly in saying *HAR-verd.* Variations such as these have been a stumbling block in designing computers that recognize spoken words, but the average human brain can adapt relatively easily to the speech of unfamiliar people and match up their phoneme variations to the generalized versions on file in the memory banks.

In addition to the units of meaning and sound (the morphemes and phonemes), the brain also stores basic frameworks or patterns into which these units fit. The framework for meaning is *grammar,* the way words are put together into meaningful sentences and their relationships to one another. Some words (*verbs*) refer to actions, while others (*nouns*) are names of people or things. *Ad-*

jectives provide descriptive details for nouns, while *adverbs* perform a similar service for verbs. There are also a variety of connecting words (*conjunctions*) and *prepositions,* which convey various kinds of relationships. In English, word order is very important to the meaning. If someone told you, "John just ate a sandwich," you might nod without much interest, but if you heard, "A sandwich just ate John," you would blink in astonishment, figuring that either you had heard wrong or you had been plunged into the middle of a science-fiction horror movie. *Word order* tells you what is acting on what and also helps to distinguish between statements and questions.

The sound units (phonemes) of a language fit into patterns of intonation and rhythm. Try saying the word *no* as though you are answering a question and being quite definite about it. Now say *no* again, but as though you are asking a question, checking to find out if something really is not so. Say it again, this time uncertainly, as though to say, "well, not exactly," or "but on the other hand. . . ." Saying that one word, the pitch of your voice changed in three characteristic tunes, or *intonations,* that would convey the same basic meanings to any English-speaking person. In some languages, such as Chinese, intonation is even more important, changing not only the basic intent of a sentence but even the meanings of individual words. The *rhythm* of a language is the pattern of stressed and unstressed syllables. Each individual English word has its own stress pattern, which sometimes can be important for its meaning. The word *contract,* for example, can be a noun meaning "an agreement" or a verb meaning "to get smaller," depending on whether the first or second syllable is stressed. When words are strung together in sentences, their individual rhythms may be slightly modified by the rhythm of the neighboring words, but the basic patterns remain the same.

When you listen to someone speaking, your brain is in a flurry of activity, constantly registering and sorting out strings of phonemes, consulting its memory banks for items in its active and passive vocabularies, and comparing the words being heard to the standard patterns of intonation, rhythm, and grammar it has on file. When you speak, the same sort of activities go on while other parts of your brain are orchestrating complicated sequences of movements of your tongue, lips, and jaws as well as your breathing muscles and larynx. A good deal of advance planning is needed in order to choose words and break them down into their phoneme sequences because all the intricate movements of the speaking apparatus must be precisely coordinated. Timing is crucial. A difference of just ten or twenty milliseconds in the moment when the vibrations of your larynx are switched on will determine whether you use a voiced or a voiceless consonant—for instance, whether you say *bit* or *pit*.

While you are speaking, your brain continually receives two kinds of feedback, relaying information on how the word making is going so far. One type is *auditory feedback,* the sound of your voice relayed up your own private pipelines, the eustachian tubes, to your ears. Nerve pathways leading from the various parts of the speech apparatus serve as another type of feedback, providing a continuous flow of backup information on the state of the muscles and the positions of the various parts—whether your lips are properly shaped for an *ee* or an *oh* sound, for example, whether your tongue is touching your teeth or the roof of your mouth, and whether your vocal cords are loosely open or stretched tight shut. This second type of feedback permits your brain to continue directing your speech even if the background noise is so loud that it drowns out the auditory feedback.

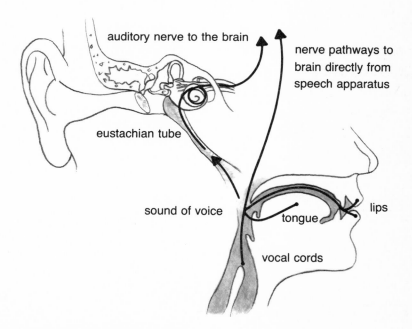

Types of feedback the brain receives during speaking.

Our knowledge of how the brain works in the understanding and formation of speech has all been gathered in a little more than a century. The first clues came from examinations of people who had suffered damage to various parts of their brains. Astute scientists, observing that certain of their functions were lost while others remained perfectly normal, deduced that the lost functions were ones controlled by the parts of the brain that had been damaged. In landmark studies during the 1860s and 1870s, a French neurologist, Paul Broca, and a German neurologist, Karl Wernicke, found that when certain areas of the *cerebral cortex* (the outer surface of the brain) were damaged, people lost the ability to speak intelligibly. The areas that they discovered, which have been named after them, are associated with different aspects of speech. *Broca's area* is concerned with the ability to put syllables together to form meaningful words. People with damage to Broca's area can still make sounds, but they are able to say only very simple words, such as *yes* or *no*. *Wernicke's area* controls the ability to understand and use symbolism; a person with damage to that part of the cortex loses not only the ability to speak, but also the ability to read, to perform mathematical calculations, and to understand the logical relationships between things.

The brain looks rather like the meat of a walnut. Its surface is marked by patterns of deep, twisting grooves and, like a walnut, its largest part, the *cerebrum* (the thinking brain), is divided into two distinct halves, or *hemispheres*. The two halves of the brain are connected

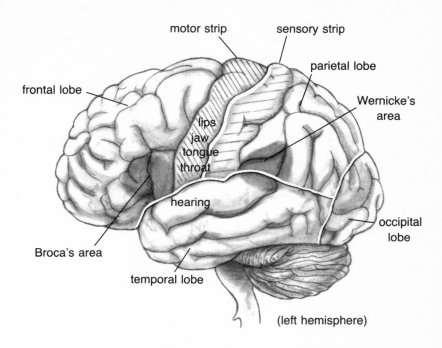

motor strip   sensory strip

parietal lobe

frontal lobe

Wernicke's
area

lips
jaw
tongue
throat

hearing

occipital
lobe

Broca's area

temporal lobe

(left hemisphere)

*The areas associated with speech have been mapped on the surface
of the cerebral cortex.*

near its base by a thick cable of about 200 million nerve
fibers. It is through this cable, called the *corpus callosum,*
that information is exchanged between the hemispheres.
Both Broca and Wernicke noticed something peculiar about
their brain-damaged patients: When the characteristic areas
in one hemisphere (usually the left) were damaged, the
ability to speak was lost. But damage to exactly the same
spots in the other hemisphere did not seem to have any
effect on speech. Studies of the brains of normal people

showed that the speech areas were better developed in one hemisphere than in the other. In the vast majority of cases, the ability for speech seemed to be centered in the left hemisphere of the brain.

During the past century or so, a great deal more has been learned about the workings of the brain in general and the areas concerned with speech in particular. This knowledge has been gathered in various ways. During operations on the brain in which the bony skull has been opened to remove a tumor or repair damage to a major blood vessel, it is possible to stimulate the brain surface directly with electrodes and observe the patient's reactions. (Brain tissue itself has no sensation of pain, so it is possible to operate on the brain or insert electrodes into it while the patient is awake, chatting with the surgeons and feeling no particular discomfort.) Stimulation of one place on the cerebral cortex may cause the patient suddenly to kick out with a foot, a tiny pulse of electricity delivered to another site may result in smacking movements of the lips, and an electrode placed in a third area may call forth a detailed memory from the patient's childhood. Another approach to revealing the brain's secrets involves the recording of *brain waves,* minute currents of electricity generated by the working brain itself. These currents can be picked up by electrodes, in the form of flat metal discs, pasted to the skin of the forehead and scalp. One of the newest techniques for brain study, the *PET scan,* involves the injection of a sugar solution tagged with a special radioactive substance in order to zero in on the parts of the brain that are working hardest during a particular activity. These varied kinds of studies have made it possible to draw up and refine maps of the brain showing where the various functions are controlled.

Studies of the brain have revealed a rather curious thing about its connections with the body: It is hooked up in a crisscross fashion, with the left hemisphere receiving sense messages from and controlling the actions of the right side of the body and the right hemisphere controlling the left half of the body. The connections to the eyes are a special variation on that theme: Nerves from the left half of the visual field of each eye feed information into the right hemisphere, while those from the right half of each visual field send information to the left hemisphere. So each hemisphere has a view of only half of what the eyes see—the half located on the opposite side from the hemisphere.

In most people, one of the brain hemispheres is a little larger and better developed than the other, and the side of the body that it controls is the dominant side. The hand on that side is stronger, better coordinated, and generally more dexterous, and there is usually a tendency to kick with the foot on that side and to depend more on the eye on that side. The majority of people—perhaps 90 percent—are right-handed, and their left hemispheres are dominant. About 95 percent of these right-handers are found to have their speech areas in the left hemisphere.

About 65 percent of left-handers also have their speech areas in the left hemisphere of the brain, but the right hemisphere controls their dominant hand. Only a small minority of left-handers show a left-hand/right-brain crisscross pattern for speech. Many left-handers have the controls for their speech abilities distributed between the two halves of their brain. So do some right-handers. In general, however, women tend to be less *lateralized* than men, meaning that they tend to have less concentration of certain types of speech abilities in one dominant hemisphere. Some researchers have suggested that competition between speech centers on both sides of the brain may explain why stuttering is more common among left-handers than among right-handers, who tend to be more lateralized. Yet girls (less lateralized) tend to develop verbal skills earlier than do boys and continue to be more verbal at all ages. If a person has a stroke that damages one of the speech areas in the cerebral cortex, less lateralization turns out to be an advantage, making it easier to regain the lost abilities as the undamaged hemisphere takes over.

Studies by a Japanese researcher, Tadanobu Tsunoda, in the 1970s suggested that the language a person learns as a child determines how the brain control areas will develop. In the brains of most Americans, Europeans, Koreans, Chinese, and Bengalis, speech sounds are processed by the left hemisphere; but animal sounds, music, and mechanical sounds such as bells, whistles, and helicopter noises are processed on the right side of the brain.

Vowel sounds are a special case: They are processed on the right side if they occur alone (for instance, the *oo* sound) but in the left hemisphere if they are combined with consonants (*boot,* for example).

The brains of Japanese and Polynesians process sounds differently. Vowels and consonants are both processed in the speech centers of the left brain, and animal sounds and Japanese music also are handled by the left hemisphere; only mechanical sounds and western music are processed in the right brain. The explanation for this is probably that in both Japanese and Polynesian languages, vowels often occur by themselves as words, and Japanese music is designed to sound like the human voice.

It is not a person's nationality but, rather, the language the person learned to speak as a child that determines how sounds are processed in the brain. Japanese-Americans brought up speaking English have the typical western lateralization, while Americans raised in Japan process vowels and other sounds on the "language side" of the brain, just as the native Japanese do.

Bilingual people, who grow up speaking two languages fluently, have larger areas of the brain devoted to speech than do people who speak only one language. That seems logical, as a person speaking two languages must be able to keep straight two different sets of vocabularies and sentence-structure rules and be able to retrieve the right word for each meaning from the two duplicate sets. Part of the speech areas in the brain is shared by the two languages, but each one also has some parts of the cortex devoted to it alone. Interestingly, the second language learned takes up a larger area in the cortex.

Much of our knowledge of brain hemispheres comes from studies of a special kind of brain-damaged patient: the *split-brain patient*. Some people suffer from severe epilepsy that cannot be controlled by drugs or other usual treatments. "Electrical storms" spread through the brains of these epileptics, producing convulsions and unconsciousness. It was found that surgically cutting the corpus callosum could stop these "electrical storms" from spreading and could thus cut off the epileptic attacks before they could develop fully. In a normal brain, there is a great deal of interchange of information from one side to the other through the nerve connections in the corpus callosum. When a person has had his or her brain "split," the two sides of the brain cannot share their incoming information.

Split-brain patients seem perfectly normal. After the operation, they can still read and write and speak. They can walk and run, bicycle, and perform various other physical tasks without any loss of balance or dexterity. Even with the nerve connections between the two halves of the brain cut, there is still plenty of opportunity for one hemisphere to find out the information that the other is receiving. The eyes seem to function normally, although each hemisphere is receiving information about only half of the field of vision. The split-brain patient is not aware that anything is wrong because the eyes move

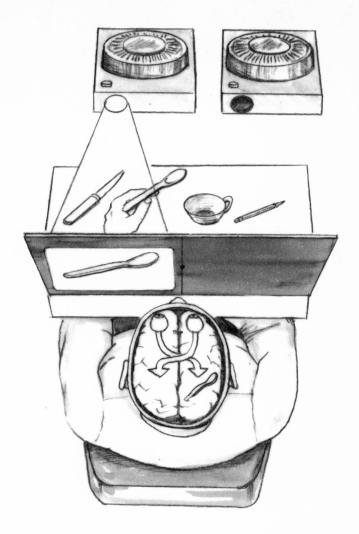

When an image of a spoon is flashed onto the left side of the screen, the split-brain subject is unable to say what the object is because the verbal left hemisphere has not "seen" anything. But the right hemisphere knows the answer and can direct the subject's left hand to pick out a spoon by touch.

constantly, zigzagging back and forth, up and down, resting for a moment on one detail and then moving on to another. The eyes move so quickly that they soon cover the whole picture, and the brain automatically fills in any gaps.

In the 1960s, Roger Sperry and his co-workers at California Institute of Technology devised a series of experiments to determine exactly what the two halves of the brain can know and do. In Sperry's experimental setup, a split-brain volunteer gazes at a spot in the middle of a screen while pictures are flashed on the screen. If a picture is flashed onto the right side of the screen and a right-handed split-brain patient is asked what object is shown, she can name it correctly without any difficulty. But if a picture is flashed onto the left side of the screen, she says, "I didn't see anything." In the first case, the information was provided to the verbal left hemisphere, the hemisphere containing the patient's speech areas. But in the second case, the information was presented only to the nonverbal right hemisphere, so the person could not name the picture verbally. Yet she could draw the object that she saw (using her left hand) or reach into a box under the table and pull out a matching object from an assortment of things.

Studies of normal people, using brain-wave recordings, PET scans, and various other techniques, have generally supported the findings of the split-brain experiments, and gradually a picture of the two halves of the brain has been assembled. In most people, the left half of the brain is the dominant hemisphere. It contains the centers for speech and for understanding language. It is strong in orderly, analytical thinking. Thus, the left brain is not only highly verbal, but also good at complicated arithmetic and problem solving. The right brain does not have much verbal ability, although it can understand simple words and do simple arithmetic; but it is good at recognizing shapes and their relationships to one another, and it has a strong artistic sense. The right brain is concerned with musical rhythm and melody, as well. It can solve problems, too, but not the way the left brain does. Instead of taking problems step by step, the right brain sees the whole picture and takes leaps of insight and intuition. It is also the side of the brain with a sense of humor. People with right-brain damage have trouble getting the punch line of a joke. They simply don't understand why it is funny and, instead, tend to analyze the joke, criticizing small details that do not really matter. Recent studies, however, suggest that negative emotions such as disgust and sadness are centered in the right hemisphere. Feelings of happiness seem to be localized in the left hemisphere.

The two halves of the brain work together in all our activities, each contributing its own special skills and complementing the other. When you listen to the news on the radio, for example, your left hemisphere is busy recognizing the commentator's words, calling up their definitions from your memory banks, and working out the meanings of the sentences. Meanwhile, the right brain is appreciating bits of humor and emotional content, fitting the new events into your general background of knowledge and experience to gain new insights, and enjoying the musical background of the commercials.

4 *How Children Learn to Talk*

What would you do if you suddenly found yourself in a strange land, where the people spoke a language you didn't understand, and no one could understand you when you tried to talk to them? How could you get food when you were hungry and a safe place to sleep when you were tired? How long do you think it would take you to puzzle out the strange sounds the natives made, to learn their names, their words for common objects and actions? How long would it take before you could talk freely with them and share ideas and emotions?

It may sound like a situation in a nightmare, but something like that has already happened to you—when you were a baby. In some ways, a baby's task is even harder than the one we have described. When you were first born, you not only could not speak the language of the people around you, but you did not even understand what a language was. You had no concept of making spoken sounds or using them as symbols for things. Even when you began to get the idea of communicating, you did not know how. You had to figure out all the rules of language for yourself, deducing them from examples that you heard. Learning to speak was probably the hardest thing you ever had to master. But you succeeded—and even enjoyed yourself while you were doing it.

Your first experiences with spoken communication began before you were born. You couldn't speak, of course, but you could hear your mother's voice and the voices of people around her. The sounds were dim and muffled—like hearing people talking through the walls of a motel room. But you could pick up the rhythms of speech, and the melody of the language became familiar. In experiments at the University of North Carolina, expectant mothers were asked to read stories aloud, several times a day, during the last weeks of pregnancy. Some of the women read *The Cat in the Hat,* by Dr. Seuss; others read *The King, the Mice, and the Cheese,* a story by Nancy and Eric Gurney. Three days after the babies were born, psychologists tested them by watching them suck on a nipple while they listened to recordings of both stories through padded earphones. The babies' sucking patterns showed that the babies whose mothers had read *The Cat in the Hat* to them before they were born preferred to hear that familiar story. The babies who had been exposed to the story by the Gurneys sucked more eagerly when they listened to that story. They remembered the rhythm and melody of the words.

Other researchers have discovered more surprising things about babies' listening abilities. When they are only four days old, babies can distinguish between sounds, even such closely related sounds as *ba* and *pa*! Psychologists at the University of Oregon determined that by measuring changes in the babies' sucking patterns as they heard new sounds.

For the first month or so, babies may be listening avidly, but they don't do much communicating on their own. Unpleasant sensations—hunger, cold, or the discomfort of a dirty diaper, for example—may set them crying. Each baby has his or her own characteristic cry, and a mother may be able to pick out her own child's voice from a whole nursery of squalling infants. Gradually, the baby's cry grows more rhythmic, resonant, and varied, so that parents may notice that one particular type of crying means hunger while another signals discomfort.

Toward the end of the first month, the baby becomes more responsive to sounds in the environment. A sudden loud sound will provoke a startle reaction, with a jerk and a gasp and the arms flung wide. The soothing sound of a chime or a mother's voice can have a quieting effect. During the second month of life, babies expand their repertoire of sounds, producing sighs and grunts and lip smackings. They begin to smile at the sight of their mother's face or the familiar sound of her voice.

After two or three months, babies begin to make pleasure sounds—melodious gurgles and coos, which delight their parents. Gradually, more vowels and consonants are added to the repertoire as the baby tries out new combinations. During this babbling stage, the baby is not really communicating, although he or she may vocalize delight-edly in response to a flow of words from a family mem-ber or baby-sitter. The baby is exploring the possibilities of the speech-making organs and practicing with them; when words like *mama* or *dada* are formed, that is gen-erally only a coincidence. Indeed, studies have shown that the young babies' babbling includes a wide variety of sounds, from virtually all the languages of the world—including some sounds that are not found in the language spoken around them. At that stage, the babies are doing some general practicing that will prepare them to learn English or French or Japanese or any other language.

In the babbling stage, listening abilities continue to outpace the baby's ability to form sounds. Researchers at the University of Washington studied six-month-old ba-bies in a specially designed experimental setting. The ba-bies sat on their parents' laps and listened to sounds broadcast through a loudspeaker. If they turned their heads to the left when they heard a change of vowel or conso-nant, a brightly lighted image of a bear would begin to dance. The babies quickly learned how to make the bear dance and demonstrated that they could distinguish vowel and consonant changes even when people with very dif-ferent voice pitches were speaking.

As the baby continues to interact with parents and oth-ers, responding to their speech with babbling, a change occurs. At some point, perhaps at the age of nine or ten months, the baby begins to imitate the sounds con-sciously, producing simple but recognizable words. The

Six-month-old babies quickly learn to turn their heads to the left to signal a change of vowel or consonant and get the dancing bear to light up.

parents respond with helpful feedback. "Yes, sweetie," the mother may say, "mama. I'm mama. That's right, mama." Researchers have observed parents interacting with their children and find that people have a special way of talking to babies. They use a gentle tone and speak more slowly than usual, in simple phrases, with a lot of repetition. These responses provide helpful cues as the baby perfects and expands a growing vocabulary.

At about this time, the baby becomes committed to a particular language—the one spoken by the adults in his or her life. Gradually, the phonemes that do not occur in this native language disappear from the baby's babbling, as a conscious effort is made to mimic the words that are heard. A research team at the University of Oregon observed the eye movements of ten-month-old babies as they responded to a woman reading in two different languages. The babies showed more interest when they heard a selection read in their native language than when they listened to a reading in an unfamiliar foreign language.

The first words that are learned are generally the names of people and things, and for some months the child uses only one word at a time. But the passive vocabulary continues to grow more rapidly than the active one, and the child can understand much more than he or she can say. During the time from twelve to eighteen months, children learn to stop what they are doing in response to a sharp "No!" They become familiar with the names of family members and common objects and can respond to simple requests. "Let's play patty cake," the mother says, and the child sits up alert and eager, with hands ready for clapping. "Where's Teddy?" "Bring me your book." "Open your mouth." Children show by their actions that they understand sentences like these, even when their speech is still limited to single words.

Somewhere between the ages of eighteen months and two years or so, when the active vocabulary has grown to perhaps two hundred words, a new stage is reached: The child begins to string two words together. Now the child has a grammar—a sort of baby grammar, consisting of a noun combined with an operator word. "More milk," the small boy demands, thrusting out his cup, and "All-gone milk," he proclaims when he has finished his second helping. "Bye-bye, Nana," calls the little girl, waving as her grandmother leaves. "Bye-bye, sock," she announces as she takes it off, and "Bye-bye, soap," she observes as the bubbly bathwater slides down the drain.

The child's first words are mainly nouns, with perhaps a couple of verbs. At the age of about two, the stock of verbs begins to expand rapidly, and gradually some adjectives and adverbs are added. Question words like *what* and *where* are useful additions. A two-year-old child may know some simple prepositions such as *to, in,* and *on* but may not be able to use words like *under* or *before*. *And* is picked up early, but other conjunctions, like *but, if,* and *though* come much later, when the child is forming complicated sentences. A two-year-old child typically refers to him- or herself by name and says things like, "Sally go out." The use of *I* and *me* comes later, and the other pronouns later still.

Young children spend many hours a day practicing words and word combinations. They murmur to themselves as they settle down to sleep, repeating bits of things they have heard and trying out variations, like "Careful, Barbara. Careful broke it. Broke the dolly. Broke the finger. Broke the vacuum clean." Soon they discover that asking questions will prompt adults to provide a wealth of additions to the growing passive vocabulary. "What's this?" they ask, again and again.

age
0–2 months   2–4 months   4–9 months   9–18 months

crying   cooing, gurgling   babbling   building phoneme system
(vocabulary mostly nouns)

18 months–
2½ years
two-word phrases,
simple questions

2½–4 years
expanding
phoneme
system,
simplified grammar

4–6 years
pronunciation mastered,
adult grammar and syntax

A child's ability to speak develops gradually, passing through a series of stages.

As the child begins to link words into combinations of three, four, and longer sequences, the word order may be a bit erratic at first. "Where you are?" a small child may ask. But gradually, listening and practicing, the child discovers the rules of adult grammar. Sometimes the process can take comic turns. Children tend to overgeneralize grammar rules at first. So when they discover that adding -*ed* to a verb shifts an action into the past, they promptly throw out all the irregular past-tense words they may already have learned, words like *saw* and *brought*. "I rided my bike," a three-year-old child may announce. He may use *mouses* as the plural for *mouse* and say *gooder* instead of *better*. As one psychologist remarked, "Leave children alone and they'll tidy up the English language." It will take more listening and perhaps some correction from parents before the child masters the more subtle points of grammar and the exceptions to the rules.

The child's phoneme system grows along with the vocabulary and grammar as the pronunciation of the various vowels and consonants is mastered. Some sounds give particular trouble, sounds such as the hissing *s* (substituting a *th* sound produces a lisp) and the *tr* combination, which may come out as *tw*. In fact, some people retain a lisp or other childish mispronunciations even as adults, either because of a speech problem or in an effort to sound "cute."

Listening ability develops much earlier than does the ability to articulate. At the age of two and a half, for example, our daughter Laura referred to her baby brother

Kevin as "Hemin." We found her version adorable and
repeated it. Laura shook her head indignantly. "Not
Hemin," she informed us. "Hemin!" She was hearing a
difference that she couldn't yet articulate. (When Kevin
first learned to talk, he reciprocated by calling his sister
"Wo-wa," which went through a stage of "Wora" before
he was finally able to pronounce all the phonemes in her
name.)

By the age of four to six, the average child has amassed
an active vocabulary of two thousand words or more and
has absorbed the basic concepts of adult grammar. The
pronunciation, intonation, and rhythm of the child's speech
are copied from those of the adults he or she has heard
speaking; usually the mother's speech has had the greatest influence.

The ages we have cited for various stages of speech
development are just averages, and there is a great deal
of individual variation. But speech experts believe that if
a child is more than six months behind these averages at
any particular stage, it may be a warning of some mental
or physical problem. In such cases, examination by a doctor or speech specialist is advisable. Many problems, such
as partial hearing loss, can be corrected. If they are not
corrected promptly, the child may never learn to speak
properly. Studies of children raised in severely deprived
environments suggest that there is a crucial stage of development, during the first few years of life, when exposure to speech is essential if a child is to learn how to
communicate properly. The child who does not receive

this kind of stimulation early enough will be unable to develop the speech areas in the brain later on. In one case, for example, a young girl was kept tied to a potty in her parents' house. Her father was an abusive man, and he hated noise. The family did not have a television set or radio, and no one spoke to her. In fact, her father and brother barked at her like dogs and hit her whenever she made a noise. The girl was rescued by a social worker when she was thirteen. By that time she had learned to keep quiet, and in the hospital to which she was taken she even threw tantrums in complete silence. Specialists worked intensively with her, trying to teach her to speak, but after years of training she still was unable to produce a complete sentence.

Fortunately, cases like these are rare. Most children are exposed to the sounds of speech throughout their development and learn to communicate almost effortlessly. We continue to add to our speaking abilities all our lives, picking up new words that are added first to our passive vocabularies and then perhaps—if they are useful words and are repeated and reinforced—to our active vocabularies.

5 Language: The Never-Ending Story

Whan that Aprille with his shoures soote
The droghte of March hath perced to the roote,
And bathed every veyne in swich licour
Of which vertu engendred is the flour;
 . . .
Thanne longen folk to goon on pilgrimages . . .

So begins one of the most famous works in the English language, *The Canterbury Tales,* by Geoffrey Chaucer.

English? you might ask. That doesn't look like English. If you could have heard people talking in the late 1300s, when Chaucer wrote his book, you would have recognized the spoken language even less.

Language is constantly changing. Our own English language is a living reflection of the past history of England and of the English people who settled other lands.

Most of the languages of Europe and some of those spoken in Asia developed from a common source: the Indo-Europeans, nomadic tribes who lived in northern-central

Europe perhaps seven thousand or eight thousand years ago. Language researchers have traced relationships among the modern Indo-European languages for many common words. *Father,* for example, is *pitar* in Sanskrit, the language of ancient India. In Latin, the language of ancient Rome, the word for father is very similar: *pater.* The German *Vater* and the French *père* come from the same common root. Another striking example is the word for brother: *bhratar* in Sanskrit, *phratar* in Greek, *Bruder* in German, *broeder* in Dutch, *brat* in Russian, and *bráthair* in Irish.

A tribe of Indo-Europeans called the Celts migrated to the British Isles long before the English arrived. The language of the Celts, Gaelic, has a lilting, melodic sound. Forms of Gaelic are still spoken today in parts of Ireland, Scotland, and Wales.

As the Roman Empire reached the height of its power, Roman legions launched a series of invasions of Britain. (The most famous one was led by Julius Caesar in 55 B.C.) Roman garrisons were set up, and some Roman words entered the local language as place-names. As it usually happens when languages cross national boundaries, local accents changed the sound of the words. The Roman *castra,* for example, meaning "camp," became *chester* in the cities of Chester, Manchester, and Winchester.

The Roman legions withdrew from Britain in A.D. 410, and Germanic tribes swept in and settled there. These tribes, the Angles, Saxons, and Jutes, spoke a language

The Roman invasion of Britain introduced some Latin words into the language of the Britons.

Viking invaders added Old Norse words to the developing English language.

rather similar to Dutch. The Celts called their German conquerors *Saxons* (or *Sassenachs*), but others gradually began to refer to them as *Anglii*. By A.D. 1000, the country was generally known as *Englaland,* the "land of the Angles." The Anglo-Saxon language formed the basis of English, and some of our most common words—*the, is, you, here, man, dog,* and *work,* for example—have Anglo-Saxon roots. But Anglo-Saxon was just the beginning of the story of English.

The next major event in the history of England and its language was the introduction of Christianity in A.D. 597. Along with a new faith, the Church introduced new words derived from Latin and Greek, such as *angel, disciple,* and *shrine.*

Toward the end of the eighth century, warlike Vikings from Norway began to raid the British coast, and some of them stayed, establishing settlements. By the middle of the ninth century, these Norse invaders, called Danes by the Anglo-Saxons, had occupied nearly half the country. King Alfred the Great stopped the advance of the Danes by a decisive military victory in 878. Trying to safeguard the peace he had won, Alfred decided to use the English language to create a sense of national identity. He rebuilt the schools and monasteries and made English the language for educating his people.

The Danes still occupied a large portion of the north of England, and their language, Old Norse, was a Germanic language like Old English. Over the generations that followed, as the Danes and the Anglo-Saxons lived side by side, words from Old Norse began to creep into the English language. Words like *get, hit, leg, low, skin, sky, want,* and *wrong* are products of the Viking invasion. But the Danes brought an even more important change to English: They helped to simplify its grammar. Old English was a highly *inflected* language. Each noun had a number of forms, in which special word endings provided meanings that we now convey with prepositions like *to, with,* and *from.* In Old English, for example, *se cyning* meant "the king," but *thaem cyninge* meant "to the king." The Viking settlers could understand many Old English words because they were similar to their Old Norse words, but the complicated grammatical inflections had no meaning for them. Over the generations, as the two peoples talked to each other in a sort of simplified common language, most of the special endings were gradually dropped. Others became more standardized, such as adding *-s* to words to make them plural.

The last major shock to the English language came with the invasion of the Normans in 1066. After the victory of William the Conqueror, the Normans took control of all the important political and religious institutions. For several generations, Norman French was the language of educated society in England. But the common people continued to speak English, and as resentment of the conquerors faded, the two peoples began to intermarry. Within a few centuries, English was again the official language of the land—now enriched by the addition of many French words.

The Renaissance in the fourteenth to seventeenth centuries brought a new flood of additions to the language. Scholars rediscovered the classics, and Greek and Latin words were borrowed. New scientific discoveries and inventions created new words, like *atmosphere, pneumonia, skeleton,* and *gravity.* Foreign trade and exploration brought in words from French, Italian, Spanish, and Dutch. (Sailors brought in such Dutch words as *smuggler* and *reef.*)

With mass communications making the world a "global community," the process of growth and change is still going on at a fast pace—not only in English but in other languages as well. Scientific terms travel from one language to another with only minor changes in spelling. French academicians fight a losing battle as they campaign for purity and try to purge their language of such Franglais terms as *le snaque-barre.* Modern technology generates a need for new terms, such as *astronaut, videocassette,* and *cloning.*

The borrowing of words from other languages and the coining of new words are only two of the ways in which language changes. Old words are taken over for new uses and gradually change their meanings. (Did you know that *nice* once meant "wanton," or "coy"?) Nouns are made into verbs, and vice versa. (We *bus* children to school.) Present-day purists who rail against the common use of *hopefully* as a dangling sentence beginner or criticize the coining of words like *finalize* lack an appreciation of the ever-changing nature of language.

Not only vocabulary but grammar can change. The distinction between *shall* and *will* seems to be on its way out, except in formal writing. Some grammatical "rules" are artificial constructions that have very little to do with the way people really use the language. Some teachers, for example, sternly caution their pupils never to split infinitives. That "rule" dates back only a century or so, when scholars decided that since infinitives are never split in Latin, they should not be split in English. The argument seems rather silly, since in Latin an infinitive such as "to hold" is a single word *(tenere)* and can't be split, whereas in English splitting an infinitive is sometimes the most logical and effective way to express a thought, and efforts to avoid it sound absurdly stilted. Language arbiters today generally advise you can feel free to split an infinitive whenever it seems to substantially improve the flow or make the meaning clearer (as it just did in this sentence).

Spoken English tends to be much less formal than the written language, discarding outmoded grammatical customs and taking shortcuts like contractions whenever possible. Strict grammarians might insist that the correct answer to the question "Who's there?" is "It is I"; but such respected speakers of English as Winston Churchill and Queen Elizabeth have been heard to say "It's me."

Spoken language varies greatly depending on who is speaking and in what circumstances. People who come from different geographical areas tend to have characteristic regional accents. The variations in the English spoken in different parts of the United States and Canada, for example, can be quite distinctive. The slow drawl of the southern states is quite different from the more clipped speech in the middle of the United States and the somewhat nasalized tones of New England. Just a word or two may be enough to identify a speaker's native region. We have learned to spot Canadian actors on television by picking up their telltale pronunciation of the word *about*. We found another example of regional differences in one of the references we consulted while writing this book. A pronunciation for the word *larynx* given as "LAIR-inks" prompted a double take and a quick trip to the dictionary, which verified that the pronunciation familiar to us— "LAR-inks"—is, indeed, the standard. Our daughter had one hypothesis to explain the discrepancy: "It must be a misprint." That seems plausible, but we came up with another possible explanation: "Maybe the author is from the midwest." When we checked the jacket flap, we found that our guess was correct.

The letter *r* seems to be a key factor in many regional accents in American English. Southerners tend to drop their *r*'s. You'd never know from listening to a Georgian, for example, that there was even one *r* in *southerner*, much less two. New Englanders tend to drop *r*'s, too, saying things like "VIG-uh" for *vigor*. But they also have a tendency to put in *r*'s where they don't belong. (President John Kennedy pronounced *Cuba* as "KYU-ber.") Dropping or adding *r*'s is a tendency shared by natives of New York ("Noo Yawk"). Unlike New Yorkers, who say "idear," a midwesterner pronounces the word *idea* more like "eye-DEE."

With modern mass communications, Americans all over the country are exposed to a "network standard" accent, the English used by newscasters. Dan Rather tells of working to eliminate the traces of his native Texan pronunciation, learning to say *ten* instead of "tin" and learning not to drop his *g*'s. "It never seems to be a problem," he says, "except sometimes when I'm tired, I tend to say *nothin'* instead of 'nothing.' " Some speech observers believe that this widespread exposure to a standard pronunciation will gradually erode regional differences and produce a more homogenized speech.

In Great Britain, the standard accent is the Received Pronunciation (RP) taught in the public schools (which in America are private schools). Great Britain, too, has many regional accents, from the London cockney dialect to the far different accents and speech patterns of northern England, as well as the Scottish burr and the Irish brogue.

When Jimmy Carter (pronounced "COT-tuh") took office as President of the United States, magazines published humorous articles purporting to educate the public in "southern-speak." Actually, however, people from different parts of the United States can generally understand each other without too much difficulty. The distinction between a regional accent and a *dialect,* a variation of a language that tends to have some differences in vocabulary and perhaps word patterns as well as in pronunciation, is rather blurred. At some point, dialects diverge so much that speakers of one have difficulty understanding those of another; ultimately, separate but closely related languages may be formed. One of us, trained as a translator of scientific Russian, can pick her way through bits of Bulgarian, Ukrainian, and other Slavic languages as well, even without any training in them.

Not only geographical regions, but social classes have their own dialects, characterized by differences in pronunciation and vocabulary. Dictionaries tend to refer to the specialized words of such dialects as "colloquial," "slang," or "vulgar," depending on how severely polite society disapproves of them. Language experts, for example, are still divided on the question of *ain't*. This word has a long history. It started out as a contraction for "am not," and it would seem to be a useful addition to the language, especially since "Am I not?" seems rather awkward in speech. (Today, "Aren't I?" is accepted in some circles, especially in Britain.) Unfortunately, *ain't* never gained the acceptance of other contractions for the verb *to be*, such as *isn't* or *aren't*, perhaps because it was associated in many people's minds with a lack of education. These days, most educated people use it sometimes (more in speech than in writing), but mainly for special emphasis or as a touch of humor. (Ain't it the truth!)

Professions also develop their own jargon or slang, and some of these specialized words may creep into the general language. *Interface, on-line, high-tech,* and *software* have already invaded the English of the masses from the growing field of computer science.

Speech differences are also signposts marking the generation gap. Teenagers are tireless inventors of *slang,* words that go into and out of fashion sometimes with head-spinning speed. The average teenager is fluently bilingual, able to converse with peers in the latest jargon and also to speak a reasonably standard version of English with parents and teachers; but there is some spillover. Some of the words that have special meanings for teenagers are readily understandable to adults (*gross,* for example) or easy to pick up. We must confess some perplexity, though, at the recent redefinition of *bad* (or should we say "baaad"?) to mean "wonderful." We're betting on "nerd" as a slang term likely to survive the test of the years, be-coming just as commonly known as *guy, okay, snafu,* and other long-lived slang words of the past.

Adults, too, are often guilty of not saying what they mean. *Euphemisms,* word substitutions that soften un-pleasant concepts, are often used. So we say someone "passes away" or a soldier "falls" in battle rather than "dies." Euphemisms are especially common in the taboo areas of sex and bodily functions, a situation that has created some difficulties for teachers, columnists, and commentators trying to warn the public about the dan-gers of AIDS and explain the precautions to be taken against this new epidemic.

An inventive way to avoid saying what you mean is rhyming slang, which has flourished in cockney English, a dialect spoken by working-class people in the East End of London, as well as in Australia. In rhyming slang, a word is replaced by a word or phrase that rhymes with it. Sometimes the slang is used as a form of euphemism: The cockney may say "in the rude" instead of *nude*. Sometimes the slang is just cheerful wordplay—for example, a suit is a "whistle and flute," and gloves are "turtledoves." Sometimes the slang has a bit of a bite to it, with cynical observations about human nature: "trouble and strife" is rhyming slang for *wife,* and "bees and honey" the phrase for *money.* Often the rhyme seems to get lost. The use of "titfer" for *hat* hardly seems like rhyming slang, but it is actually a shortened version of "tit for tat." The slang word *khyber* as a euphemism for backside (ass) came from British soldiers stationed at Khyber Pass.

With enough rhyming-slang words thrown in (particularly ones that have dropped the rhyming part), the speech becomes a sort of secret language, which people can use to converse in while hiding their meaning from outsiders. Cockney also includes a number of other "in-group" devices, such as shortenings of phrases ("gorblimey" is actually a contraction of "God blind me") and borrowings of words from a variety of sources, from *shufti* (a Hindustani word meaning "a look around") to "parlyvoo" ("a talking session," from the French *parlez-vous*), *pal* (the now-common word for "friend" that was originally a word in the Romany language of the Gypsies), and various Yiddish words such as *shemozzle* ("confusion"), *gelt* ("money"), and *nosh* ("food"). *Back slang* is another kind of secret language, formed by pronouncing words backward and used by London street traders since the mid-nineteenth century. "Yob," meaning "boy," is the best-known back-slang word. ("Yobbo" comes from the Irish *boyo*.) Traders find secret codes for the numbers especially useful: In back slang, for example, *one* becomes "eno," and *four* is "rouf."

Codes and secret languages are popular among many groups. Schoolchildren enjoy exchanging messages in pig Latin, a simple code produced by removing the initial consonant of a word, tacking it onto the end of the word, and adding *-ay*. *Pig Latin* thus becomes "igpay atinlay" in pig Latin. In certain religions, the use of ancient languages such as Latin or Hebrew for rituals serves both to preserve tradition and to build a sense of community and exclusiveness. (The modern trend in many sects, though, is to translate church rituals into the language of the country, so that people can understand and participate more readily.)

Families may develop a kind of coded language not readily understood by outsiders, using words derived from their ethnic background or phrases that arose in some memorable family incident. Twins often develop an especially close bond and may speak a unique code language understandable only to each other. Speech pathologists have been studying the private language of a pair of twins in California, Grace and Virginia Kennedy. Gracy and Ginny grew up under somewhat unusual circumstances that promoted an unusually close bond between them. Their family was having money problems when they were born and could afford only one crib at first; so for six months the two girls shared everything, including a crib. Those six months were filled with other problems, too. Both babies suffered from violent convulsions. Electroencephalograms of their brain-wave patterns, taken when they were a year old, were normal, but the doctors told their parents that Gracy and Ginny might be slightly retarded. The Kennedys both had to work at full-time jobs to support the family, and the twin girls were cared for by their grandmother, who didn't have much time to talk to them or teach them games. When they were three years old, the twins were still making their needs known by single words or gestures. Their parents assumed that their slowness in learning to talk was evidence that they were, indeed, mentally retarded. The family moved at that time to a neighborhood populated mainly by senior citizens. With few other playmates of their own age, Gracy and Ginny continued to spend most of their time together, retreating into their own private little world. When speaking to their parents, they rarely said more than a word or two at a time—useful phrases like "want water" or "me juice." They didn't speak in sentences, even when they were old enough to go to school. Yet when the twins were alone together, they chattered animatedly, rattling off words at a fantastic rate. The problem was that their words weren't understandable to anyone else.

The Kennedys assumed that their twin daughters were talking mostly gibberish, strings of meaningless sounds, although they noticed that the girls had made up nicknames for each other. Gracy was "Poto," and Ginny was "Cabengo." When the girls were six and a half, their parents consulted speech experts at the Speech, Hearing and Neurosensory Center in San Diego. Speech pathologists there made audio- and videotape recordings of the girls' play and discovered that their strange-sounding sentences, like "Cabengo padem manibadu peetu," had consistent meanings. Some of their words seemed to be strings of phonemes that they had invented themselves for communicating in their own private language (which they spoke only to each other). Other words seem to have developed from a young child's typical mispronunciations of spoken English words. The twins' word for *finish,* for example, was "pinnit"; the word they used for *vehicle,* "gamba," came from the family's camper. In addition to taping play sessions of the twins alone, the therapists also worked intensively to teach the girls Standard English, and they began to attend regular classes in school. They were placed in separate classes to encourage them to play and talk with other children. Gracy and Ginny responded quickly to all the attention and began to master the details of vocabulary, sentence structure, and word order. The therapists concluded that the twins were not retarded at all; their seizures apparently had had no permanent effect, and they were slow to develop normal speech merely because of a lack of stimulation. Meanwhile, studies of their private language are bringing insights into this curious phenomenon, which specialists refer to as *idioglossia.*

Another unusual kind of speech is *glossolalia,* or "speaking in tongues." Since biblical times, some religious people have claimed that divine inspiration causes them to speak long and fluent passages of unintelligible sounds. Sociologist Nicholas Spanos, however, believes that glossolalia is taught to converts and consists of nonrandom patterns of vowels and consonants that have no real meaning. Spanos has taped Pentecostal Protestants speaking in tongues and then replayed one-minute segments of their speech to people who had never heard it before. When asked to mimic it (without reproducing it exactly), about one-fifth of the volunteers were immediately able to do so. In some religious groups, new members are told to listen carefully to glossolalic speakers and to practice the sounds silently. When Spanos tried this technique with volunteers, 70 percent of them were able to learn to speak fluently in tongues. The suspicion that glossolalic experiences may not really be evidence of divine inspiration is not new. Even the Apostle Paul, who spoke in tongues himself, felt that understanding was the important thing. "I would rather speak five words with my mind, in order to instruct others," he said, "than ten thousand words in tongues."

6 *Meanings in the Message*

Do lie detectors really work? This question has taken on considerable importance in today's world, where many government agencies and private companies have set up programs of routine lie-detector screening of employees and job applicants.

The *polygraph*, or lie detector, is a high-tech method designed to reveal whether what people say is really what they believe to be true. Sensitive pickups record changes in blood pressure, the galvanic potential of the skin (a measure of sweating), muscle contractions, and other physiological changes that are indications of tension. The theory is that the emotional conflict set up by telling a lie will give rise to such physiological changes. Studies show, however, that the interpretation of lie-detector tests depends greatly on the skill and experience of the operator, and even with an expert polygraphist there is a substantial margin of error. An innocent person may show signs

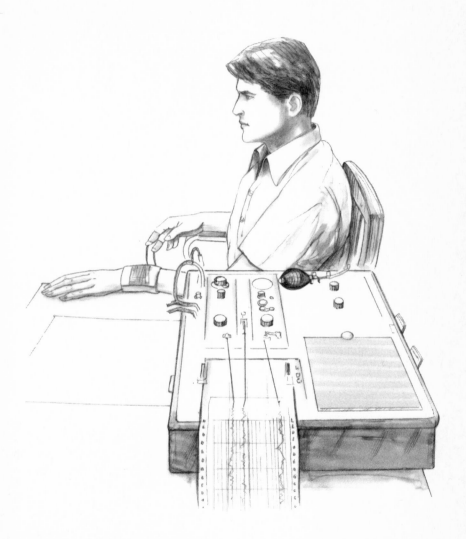

The polygraph supposedly detects lying by measuring physiological changes associated with stress.

of emotional tension while telling the truth because of fear, whereas a practiced liar may have little or no emotional reaction to telling untruths. Typically, lie-detector tests catch about 80 percent of liars, but they are only about 60 percent accurate in identifying people who are telling the truth. In a sample of 1,000 people, let us say, 50 of whom are lying while the other 950 are telling the truth, the lie detector will catch about 40 of the liars, letting 10 slip away. But only 570 of the truth-tellers will test innocent, and 380 will be wrongly accused of lying!

Even without the high-tech trappings of the polygraph, speakers provide a number of clues to the truthfulness or deception of their words. Speech is accompanied by a complex *body language,* which includes facial expressions, posture, and a variety of gestures. Fidgeting and avoiding eye contact are popularly thought to be indications of lying. Actually, however, they may merely indicate that the speaker is uncomfortable, whereas a practiced liar has learned to look people in the eye and stay calm. Liars often do make gestural slips, such as a barely noticeable shrug of one shoulder, the lifting of an eyebrow, or the rotating of a hand. Body gestures and facial expressions may not match when a person is lying, or they may be slightly out of sync. Facial expressions that last more than four or five seconds may be put on to deceive, and lopsided expressions (unless they are a habitual mannerism) may be indications of lies. When films of a person speaking are rerun in slow motion, they often reveal *microexpressions*—fleeting expressions that last for only a fraction of a second—that reveal emotions quite different from those the speaker is trying to display. For example, a fleeting expression of rage may briefly interrupt a smile.

When we converse, we constantly take in and evaluate not only the speaker's words, but also the fine shadings of meaning added by the speaker's body language. Curiously enough, some of this nonverbal language comes through even when we cannot see the speaker. Rutgers University psycholinguist Vivien Tartter has found that 80 percent of the time, listeners over the telephone can tell if an unseen speaker is smiling. The movement of the facial muscles reshapes the sounds of speech in ways we can interpret. Other telephone studies have focused on the effectiveness of telephone sales. It was found that when normally effective salespeople winked, smirked, smiled, or slouched in their seats while making a telephone presentation, listeners tended to distrust them. When the same telephone salespeople were seated at neat desks, in comfortable chairs, in a well-lit room without distractions, their sales efficiency was high.

Speech itself provides a number of clues to meaning in addition to those provided by the words. Shifts of intonation can drastically change the meaning of a sentence, transforming a simple declaration into a question or an expression of disbelief, scorn, or anger. The pitch of people's voices tends to rise when they are under stress (that's another not-always-reliable sign of lying), and excitement or uneasiness may make a person talk faster. Differences in speech style, speed, and mannerisms are partly determined by the local culture. Regional telephone companies use recorded messages in a style that will be comfortable for their subscribers. A telephone number supplied by Los Angeles directory assistance takes an average of fifteen seconds to play, whereas a New York recording averages only ten seconds. The speeds of the messages are consciously selected to suit the slower, more "laid-back" California style and the faster pace of life in New York. Such differences may cause misunderstandings between people from different regions. Southerners in conversation, for example, show politeness by pausing, whereas New Yorkers are used to faster-paced conversations with frequent interruptions. If an Alabaman and a New Yorker are talking, the southerner may wait vainly for a pause in the conversation and find the fast-talking northerner rude; the New Yorker, meanwhile, wonders if the Alabaman is just too slow-witted to speak up.

A person's sex can also make a difference in patterns of speech and conversation. Linguists and sociologists who have tape-recorded and studied hundreds of conversations have discovered that women ask about three times as many questions as men and are much more likely to open a conversation with a question. Women's speech tends to be much more animated in general. Changes in intonation are used to emphasize particular words, and intensifier words, like *so* and *such*, are frequently thrown in. ("Guess what I saw today? A *deer*! Right out in the *road*, in broad *day*light! I was so surprised, just completely *flabber*gasted!" A sociolinguist would have no difficulty guessing the sex of the speaker in that conversation opener.) Women typically have more effective conversational skills. They listen more attentively and are more likely to offer supporting responses like "Really? What happened?" that help to draw the other person out and keep the conversation moving along. Men often fail to respond or may answer in noncommittal monosyllables, such as "Hmm" or "Yeah." Some studies have shown that men are much more likely to interrupt another speaker—particularly if the other speaker is a woman. The researchers theorize that these different conversational styles reflect male-female power relationships and note that both sex and status play a role. In one study of conversations between doctors and their patients, it was found, as expected, that patients interrupted doctors much less often than doctors interrupted patients. But female doctors were interrupted more often when they had male patients.

What is the significance of slips of the tongue? Are they just unimportant accidents, minor malfunctions of the speech mechanisms? Or do they hold some hidden meaning?

Pioneering psychoanalyst Sigmund Freud believed that in verbal slips we inadvertently reveal our hidden motives and anxieties. "I'm unhappy to meet you. I mean, happy!" you blurt out after an introduction, leaving everyone wondering about your true feelings. "Could I be excused from the exam?" a student asks. "My grandmother just lied. I mean, died." The teacher murmurs condolences, meanwhile wondering if it was really the student who was lying.

Recent studies by psycholinguist Michael Motley of the University of California at Davis suggest that at least some verbal errors might well be classic "Freudian slips." In one of his experiments, three groups of thirty male students each were asked to read pairs of words on a computer screen. Students in all three groups read along silently until a buzzer sounded; then they had to read the next pair of words aloud. Students in the first group had electrodes attached to them, and they were told that at some point in the experiment they would receive a powerful electric shock. (Actually, the electrodes were not connected to a source of current, but the student volunteers did not know that and went through the entire experiment worrying about when they would receive a shock.) Students in the second group did not have electrodes attached; the experiment was conducted by a seductive-looking young woman. Students in the third group served as "controls": They performed their reading task under the supervision of a male researcher, without any electrodes or other distractions. Students in the first group tended to make verbal slips that revealed their particular anxiety: They misread "damn shock" for the words "sham dock" on the screen and said "cursed wattage" instead of "worst cottage" twice as often as did students in the control group. The student volunteers in the second group revealed that the sexy female researcher was influencing their thoughts: They read out "fast passion" instead of "past fashion" and said "happy sex" for "sappy hex," also twice as often as did the controls.

Although some verbal errors do seem to have hidden meanings, it is likely that many slips of the tongue are merely slips of the tongue—or of other parts of the speech-making apparatus. Speaking is a very complex task, requiring precise control and coordination. The brain must plan ahead, a number of words in advance, to keep the actions of the larynx, tongue, jaws, and lips in the proper sequence and synchronization. When you try to pronounce a tongue twister like "She sells seashells by the seashore" or "Peter Piper picked a peck of pickled peppers," you quickly discover how difficult it is to keep the words flowing smoothly when small but precise differences must be articulated in quick succession.

The brain constantly monitors speech through auditory feedback and puts in corrections when errors are detected. One common type of verbal slip involves the misplacing of parts of words, most often the initial consonants. The brain, racing ahead, may accidentally set up the wrong consonant for a word and then, realizing it, compensate by an even switch, substituting the missing phoneme for the one that was already used. This kind of slip, which may produce some very amusing results, is called a *spoonerism*, named after an Oxford don named William Spooner. The Reverend Doctor was well known for switching consonants and sometimes whole words. Spooner's most famous blooper was a reference to Queen Victoria as "the queer old dean" instead of "the dear old

Queen." He once addressed a group of farmers as "noble tons of soil" instead of "noble sons of toil" and remarked that "work is the curse of the drinking classes" when he meant to say "drink is the curse of the working classes." (Could there be a bit of Freudian slip in some of Dr. Spooner's spoonerisms?) The Reverend Doctor outdid himself in one speech expelling a failing student from his courses: "You have hissed all my mystery lectures. You have tasted the whole worm and must leave by the first town drain."

Another common type of verbal slip is word substitution. In the particular variety called *malapropism,* named after Mrs. Malaprop, a character in an eighteenth-century play who had this type of speech problem, the word that is substituted sounds somewhat like the correct word but is hilariously inappropriate. One of humorist Erma Bombeck's favorite columns tells about her young son's speech problems. He came home one day and reported the teacher said he had trouble with his "bowels," and on another occasion he told his class at school that his mother was a "syndicated communist."

Malapropisms are typically the result of a lack of education, but other word-substitution slips are due to slip-ups in the brain's filing and retrieval system and provide valuable insights into the mental processes of language. Linguist Victoria Fromkin has collected and analyzed more than fifteen thousand verbal slips and found that they fit into definite patterns. Words are apparently classified in the brain according to sound, meaning, and grammar.

When we slip and accidentally pull out the wrong word, the substitutions follow definite rules. Generally a noun is substituted for a noun, a verb for a verb, an adjective for an adjective, and so forth. We may misretrieve a word from the same general category, saying, for example, "My tongues were bleeding" instead of "My gums were bleeding." (In that slip, a little similarity of the sounds might help to promote the confusion.) Substitution of antonyms is another common slip—for example, saying *up* instead of *down* or *increase* instead of *decrease*. Sometimes two related words or two synonyms may be pulled out at the same time and combined, producing such inventive hybrids as "splisters" for *splinters* and *blisters* or "smever" for *smart* and *clever*.

A current psycholinguistic theory known as *spreading activation* neatly explains both Freudian slips and the accidental "slips of the tongue." A person's mental dictionary is thought to be organized so that each word is interconnected with other words, associated by meaning, sound, or grammar. The complex interconnections are similar to an intricate spiderweb. When we are preparing to speak, the appropriate parts of the web are activated. The activation spreads, first to the most closely related words and then to words associated with them. Both the particular situation and the undercurrent of thoughts and feelings may be included in the web of associations. Reverberations spread through the web as each word activates an alternate path. The point in the web (that is, the word) that accumulates the greatest activation is selected.

If two competing choices have equal or nearly equal activation levels, a verbal slip may occur.

The spreading-activation theory can account for many slips in everyday speech. In our family, for example, as in many families with a number of children, we often find ourselves calling a child by the wrong name. Our slips seem to follow definite patterns. We almost never confuse the boys' names with the girls' names (we have three of each), and the names we switch most frequently are those of our sons Glenn and Kevin. Poor Kevin, our youngest, answers uncomplainingly to "Glenn"; he reports that even the teachers at school often call him that. He can take consolation in the fact that we call Glenn "Kevin" nearly as often as the reverse, and sometimes we come up with hybrids like "Kenn" or "Glevin." Both boys are whizzes at math and science and are active in sports, similarities that may account for part of the confusion in our mental cataloging. The sounds of their names are also somewhat similar and quite different from the name of their older brother, Bob.

Linguistics researcher Elaine Chaika finds explanations in the current linguistic theories for the bizarre and disjointed speech characteristic of schizophrenics. Some psychiatrists believe that people suffering from this form of mental illness speak strangely to express and at the same time hide feelings that are socially unacceptable. Their bizarre and poetic-sounding speech patterns are metaphors for deeper meanings, they say, and it is the task of the therapist to find those meanings. But Chaika finds simpler explanations in psycholinguistics. She cites an example of a patient who was asked to identify a color chip:

"Looks like clay," the patient said. "Sounds like gray. Take you for a roll in the hay. Hay day. Mayday. Help. I need help."

Was this a poetically phrased cry for help? Chaika believes that it was more likely a process of association, very similar to the kind that occurs in verbal slips. The schizophrenic patient's attention was momentarily caught by a series of chance rhymes, finally ending in a translation of *Mayday* into its common meaning, a cry for help. Typically, the schizophrenic does not have the automatic monitoring and correction of speech that "normal" people have. The patient fails to suppress chance associations and, instead of sticking to one topic, wanders randomly along. Linguist Eugene Nida noted that his schizophrenic friend's speech seemed to be disrupted at different levels, depending on how well his mental disorder was being controlled. First his general organization of speech started to break down, then rules for sentences as he began to string words together on the basis of association rather than sense. That was followed by, first, inappropriate use of words and, finally, *gibberish*—groups of nonsense syllables that Elaine Chaika refers to as "word salad." Nida found that he could almost tell how many days his friend had skipped taking his medication by noting to which level his speech had degenerated. This kind of consistent correlation between the type of speech degeneration and the degree of mental illness is not always observed, however. Some schizophrenics cycle back and forth from one level to another during speech.

The causes of the disordered speech of schizophrenics may lie in the biochemistry of the brain. Drugs such as Thorazine, used to treat this mental illness, restore more normal thought processes and lessen the speech disorders as well.

7 _Speech Problems_

Speech specialists estimate that about one out of ten people in the United States suffers from some kind of communication disorder. These disorders range from a mild speech impairment such as a childish lisp to a complete inability to produce meaningful sounds, and their causes are just as varied.

One of the most common causes is hearing loss. This may be the result of damage to structures of the ear (the noise of an amplified rock band at a dance, for example, can have a devastating effect on the delicate hair cells in the inner ear that normally operate in receiving sounds) or impairment of the areas of the brain involved in receiving and processing sounds. Often hearing loss is only partial, involving a reduction of the volume of sounds or a loss of certain frequencies, such as the higher-pitched sounds. Human speech normally has a great deal of built-in _redundancy_, extra clues that help the hearer to guess parts of what the speaker is saying, on the basis of word patterns and meaning, even if not everything is heard clearly. (Telephone systems take advantage of this redundancy: The lines transmit less than half of the frequency range of the human voice, so that high- and low-pitched sounds are lost; yet we can usually understand what people are saying well enough.) If speech is too faint to hear, however, or key parts of words are missed, listening becomes a complete guessing game, and the effectiveness of communication breaks down.

When hearing loss occurs in later years, after a person has learned to speak fluently, there may be little effect on speech. But when a child is born deaf or suffers a hearing loss at a very young age, special techniques may be needed to teach the child to speak at all. The special problems of speech for the deaf will be discussed in Chapter 9. The important thing to emphasize here is that it is vital to diagnose children's hearing problems as early as possible. At a few months of age, deaf children babble spontaneously, just as children with normal hearing do. But after a while, when normally babbling becomes less spontaneous and more a response to the speech children hear, the deaf child's babbling fades away. That should be a cue for parents to take the child to a specialist for evaluation; hearing and communication problems can be diagnosed as early as six months of age.

A young baby with a hearing loss can be fitted with a hearing aid that amplifies sound. The parents and others who care for the child should talk to the child, play games that stimulate responses, and accompany their activities with spoken words just as they would—or even more than they would—with a normally hearing child. Taking care to speak loudly, slowly, and clearly may help to provide the hearing-impaired child with the kind of language input that helps the speech areas of the brain to develop.

Parents naturally tend to compare their children's development with that of other children in the family or neighborhood. Such comparisons can sometimes produce a lot of envy and unhappiness. But they can be useful in helping to spot health or emotional problems that may be treatable. Children are individual in their speech development, just as they are in other areas, and no two children will follow exactly the same patterns in mastering this important human skill. But as a general rule, when a child lags substantially behind the average development for the age, it is a good idea to check with a doctor.

Mental retardation is one of the main causes of delays in learning to speak. In some spastic conditions, such as cerebral palsy, the child's intelligence may be perfectly normal or even superior, but an inability to control the muscles prevents the development of normal speech. (The invention of typewriters with specially modified controls for handicapped people has opened up a whole new world of communication for those who suffer from such conditions.) Prolonged illness or a severe accident may set back a child's development both in speech and in other areas. Malfunction of one of the endocrine glands, resulting in an insufficient production of key hormones, may make a child sluggish and dull and slow to acquire speech. Lack of enough speech stimulation can be another key factor—

we learn to speak by imitating those who speak to us and through the give-and-take of communicating with them. A child who doesn't hear enough speech will not learn to speak well.

Some children master the fundamentals of speech and learn vocabulary at a normal rate but have persistent problems of articulation. Errors of pronunciation are common as a child is learning to form phonemes and words. Saying "widdo" for *little* and "thoup" for *soup* can be very cute at the age of two or three; but a child who is still using such "baby talk" by school age may be in for an unmerciful teasing by classmates. Generally, children can produce all the vowels correctly about 90 percent of the time by the age of two and a half, and their mastery of the consonants is 90 percent correct by four and a half. Speech specialist Irene Poole lists the following ages for the mastery of the various consonants:

At 3½	*b, p, m, w, h*
At 4½	*d, t, n, g, k, ng, j, y*
At 5½	*f*
At 6½	*v, th(the), z, s, sh, l*
At 7½	*s, zh, r, th(thin), hw*

Consonant blends, like *pl*, *bl*, and *sp*, are mastered last of all.

A failure to achieve language fluency on schedule may be the result of overprotection or constant anticipating of the child's needs so that he or she has no motivation to learn how to communicate. Frequent ear infections or excess wax in the ears may prevent a young child from hearing the fine distinctions of phonemes clearly enough to imitate them correctly. Special exercises under the supervision of a speech therapist can help the child learn to communicate more effectively.

Speech pathologist Samuel Fletcher at the University of Alabama has recently invented two electronic devices to help people with speech problems to master the fine distinctions of pronunciation. The *palatometer* is an aid to learning consonants, and the *glossometer* helps in the mastery of vowels. Each consists of a thin, custom-fitted mouthpiece that hugs the roof of the mouth and contains electronic sensors that relay information on the tongue's position to a computer. The palatometer's sensors respond to touch and can make fine distinctions: between *s* and *sh*, for example. The glossometer bounces light off the tongue to photosensors and traces the height and shape of the tongue as it forms vowel sounds. A person working with the devices watches a computer screen, where an outline of the sound produced is compared to the correct pattern for the consonant or vowel sound. These new speech learning aids are particularly valuable for the deaf and for people with speech impediments that make it difficult to form certain sounds. In an early test of the system, two deaf children and one with a speech impediment were able to produce a recognizable *s* sound in about ten minutes, although they had been unable to learn it before.

A birth defect called *cleft palate* occurs in about one

out of a thousand children. The bones of the *palate* (the roof of the mouth) do not form completely and fail to grow together, resulting in a gap. (The child may also have a cleft lip, or *harelip*.) Since the mouth and lips are important in forming the sounds of speech, a child with a cleft palate cannot articulate clearly. Fortunately, this is a condition that is fairly easy to correct surgically. The surgery should be performed as early as possible so that the child will be able to learn to speak properly. After the defect is corrected, a speech therapist works with the child, helping to develop good speech habits.

A common speech problem is *stuttering*, or *stammering*, a faulty form of speech repeatedly broken by hesitations, interruptions, or repetitions of sounds or syllables. "That's all, f-f-f-f-f-folks" may sound funny when a cartoon character says it, but that kind of articulation problem can be a nightmare of embarrassment to a habitual stutterer. When a child is first learning to speak, a certain amount of stammering is perfectly normal. The child has a flood of ideas to express, with only a limited vocabulary and an incomplete mastery of the mechanics of speech. The small child starts to say something, hesitates to grope for a word or to fix up one that wasn't coming out right, and makes a fresh start. This kind of stammering is especially common between the ages of two and four. It becomes a problem when parents or friends call attention to it, perhaps advising the child, "Now, take a deep breath, slow down, and think about what you want to say." Soon, instead of being automatic, speech has become a cumbersome chore and an emotional ordeal. The greater the stress, the more likely the child is to stumble on the words and the more worry and stress this new failure creates.

Researchers have tried, so far unsuccessfully, to trace hereditary origins of stuttering or to find neurological or biochemical differences between stutterers and nonstutterers. It seems likely that some people have more of a tendency to stutter than others, but actually developing this kind of speech problem seems to be the result of some triggering stress in the child's environment. The stress of competing with other children for a parent or teacher's attention may be such a triggering factor. Or the child may be reacting to some emotionally upsetting situation, such as the bitter arguments of parents heading for a divorce.

For people whose stuttering problems have become firmly established, a variety of techniques can be helpful. Most of them involve forms of distraction, and they seem to work by preventing the stutterer from tuning in on his or her own speech through the usual auditory feedback. (Stutterers seem to stutter mainly when they hear themselves stutter.) Wearing a headphone that feeds in a distracting "white noise" is one way to stop stuttering. Some techniques have the stutterer talk in rhythm with a metronome or while walking with arms swinging. The great Greek orator Demosthenes is said to have cured himself of stuttering by practicing speaking with a mouthful of pebbles. The effort of forming words clearly around the impediment of the pebbles provided the necessary distraction from his problem. Other famous stutterers have included Moses, Winston Churchill, Marilyn Monroe, and Raymond Massey (who could speak fluently when he acted a role but not in his everyday life). Curiously, most stutterers lose the telltale hesitations when they are alone, when they talk to pets, when they read aloud, and when they sing.

When you are talking with someone who stutters, try to act normally. As in any polite conversation, wait for the stutterer to finish his or her sentences without interrupting or supplying words. Don't yield to the temptation to look away in embarrassment, either. Signs of your impatience or discomfort will only make the stutterer tenser and less able to control the problem. An estimated two-and-a-half million Americans stutter. Many of them, trying to avoid humiliation and anxiety, get into the habit of avoiding situations that would require them to speak with other people—they reject jobs involving conversation, don't date or go to parties, and are afraid even to ask directions or make a phone call. Help for these sufferers is provided by the National Stuttering Project, an organization that publishes newsletters and sponsors self-help groups in every state. Sample materials can be obtained by sending a self-addressed, stamped envelope (two stamps) to National Stuttering Project, 1269 Seventh Avenue, San Francisco, CA 94122.

A variety of communication problems can result from damage to the brain. Specialized areas of the brain control the reception and interpretation of spoken words, the formation and selection of words, and the physical movements of the various parts of the speaking apparatus. A *stroke,* blockage or bursting of one of the blood vessels supplying the brain, may cut off the vital supply of oxygen and food materials to brain cells. These delicate cells can die after only a four-minute interruption of their blood supply, and then the functions in which they were involved may be impaired. Head injuries, especially those resulting from car or motorcycle accidents, can cause massive brain damage, which, in turn, may affect the speech functions. Drug abuse is another possible cause of communication problems: Common "street drugs," such as PCP, glue fumes, and cocaine, can cause brain damage, and so can America's legal drug of choice, alcohol. Brain damage can also result from a serious illness such as meningitis.

When we think of someone who has lost the ability to speak as a result of brain damage, we tend to picture an elderly stroke victim in a nursing home. But strokes can hit young people, too, and accidents and drug abuse are frequent causes of injury among teenagers and young adults. Speech therapist Jan Snavely of southern California has discovered that about one-third of juvenile offenders suffer from learning, speech, and hearing problems. Many of them have histories of drug use, or head injuries from gang violence, family arguments, or car accidents. Snavely has set up a program of therapy for communication problems, teaching basic language skills and working on more effective eye contact and facial expressions. Her pioneering program and others patterned after it are helping these troubled young people to become better able to cope in the everyday world of jobs and family living after their release.

The various kinds of language disorders due to damage or malfunction of speech areas in the brain are grouped under the general term *aphasia*, which can be defined as the ability to put into symbols the things one knows or the inability to understand other people's symbols. There are a number of different forms of aphasia, among them:

Wernicke's aphasia. The person speaks fluently in what sounds like sentences and words with normal intonation, but the words are gibberish and don't make any sense. A person with this kind of aphasia, intending to comment about the weather, might say something like, "The bun is brindling, but it may dram tomorrow."

Broca's aphasia. Speech is labored and slow. It leaves out little words, like a telegram, but still makes sense.

Anomia. The person can speak relatively normally but can't remember the names of people or objects. Reaching a noun in a sentence, the anomic hesitates, groping for a word, and may talk around it, defining it until the listener understands or guesses what is meant. Shown a comb and asked to name it, an anomic may say, "You smooth out your hair with it."

Conduction aphasia. The person can understand what is said and can say what he wants to say but cannot repeat things that are said to him.

Isolation aphasia. The person can repeat anything that is said but can't put words together to form new messages and thus cannot communicate effectively with others.

Brain disorders can also produce other kinds of speech problems. There may be a disconnection from the person's own feelings, and patients may speak of themselves in the third person. Words with strong associations in the brain's memory banks may be confused—the person may say "dog" instead of "cat" or "no" when "yes" is meant. Words with similar sounds may be confused, such as *chief* and *cheap* or *cheapskate* and *cheesecake*.

Have we started you searching back over your own recent conversations and worrying about possible brain damage? Don't worry. Everyone makes these kinds of speech mistakes occasionally, especially when tired or upset. People with particular types of brain damage make them regularly.

Damage to the motor area of the brain can result in another kind of speech problem: *dysarthria*, the inability to articulate words. Normal people suffer from some degrees of dysarthria when they are drunk; they slur their words and are unable to make fine distinctions among phonemes. "Jush a minnit," a drunk might say, instead of "just a minute." Alcohol, depressing the action of the brain's nerve cells, mimics (fortunately, temporarily) the effects of brain damage on speech as well as other types of motor coordination.

Therapy for brain-damaged patients is highly individual, tailored to the needs of each patient, but it can be very effective. Other areas of the brain can learn to take over for the damaged areas, and often full speech abilities are restored. Movie actress Patricia Neal suffered a stroke as a young adult, at the height of her career. Although the damage to her brain produced severe aphasia, intensive speech therapy and determined practice made her able to resume her acting career successfully.

Some people with aphasia are unable to form words in normal speech but, when angry or upset, can swear fluently. Brain researchers speculate that swearing and other normally suppressed language materials may be stored separately in the brain or processed differently from the language used in everyday communication. These speculations are supported by observations of people with a rare hereditary condition called *Tourette's syndrome*. Tourette sufferers have normal intelligence but are sometimes seized by involuntary tics, which may take the form of violent blinking, muscle twitches, or uncontrollable verbal outbursts: grunts, shrieks, or sudden outpourings of curse words. The uncertainty of never knowing when you are going to embarrass yourself by suddenly twitching or shouting out obscenities puts an enormous emotional strain on Tourette victims, who may find it difficult to hold jobs and maintain relationships. (One of them tells of receiving forty-two W-2 forms, each from a separate job, in a single year.) Tourette's syndrome is currently thought to be the result of a defect in the transmission of messages among the brain's nerve cells. Drugs such as haloperidol are helping many of these victims.

One of the most puzzling and tragic of communication disorders is called *autism*. Autistic children seem to live in a private dream world, avoiding contact with others. They develop good motor control but may spend hours in repetitive actions like rhythmic rocking or head banging. They are unresponsive, often from earliest babyhood. They do not respond to people's faces or voices or to being picked up and cuddled. Some autistic children never learn to speak; others may speak fluently but do not use speech to communicate. They may repeat songs or poems after a single hearing, showing an exceptional auditory memory; sometimes they tend to echo the last few words of someone else's sentence (a speech disorder called *echolalia*). But their spontaneous speech seems to be generated by a complex inner life rather than by their interactions with other people. Their voices are high-pitched and monotone, lacking expression. Often, they use words extremely literally or take a word or phrase from one situation and use it inappropriately in another. (One autistic child said "don't throw the dog off the balcony" to indicate "no.") They may reverse pronouns, saying "you" instead of "I," or may confuse parts of the body, for example, complaining "bumped the head" when some other part of the body was hurt.

Between one hundred thousand and two hundred thousand children and adults in the United States suffer from autism. There are various theories as to how autistic children should be treated. Some approaches use rewards and punishments to reinforce behavior that is responsive to other people. Sometimes an autistic child forms an attachment to a teacher or caretaker, and that can serve as the beginning of a long and complicated therapy. Some drugs used to treat mental illness are also showing promise in the treatment of autism. At least some autistics have been found to have an excess of the neurotransmitter dopamine in their brains, and the standard schizophrenia drug haloperidol, which works by blocking the action of dopamine, seems to work in autism, too. But haloperidol can produce serious side effects, and doctors are reluctant to use it for long-term treatment of children. A newer drug, fenfluramine, is now being tested in about two dozen centers in the United States and Canada. It seems to improve an autistic child's learning ability, in addition to normalizing behavior.

Linguist Laura Meyers of the University of California at Los Angeles has been working with a group of teenagers with *Down's syndrome,* the most common form of mental retardation. Children with this hereditary condition have tongues that are longer than usual, making it difficult to form words clearly, and they seem unable to hear or understand the small words that give structure to a sentence. Their speech seems telegraphic: "Cat. Jump. Chair," for example, instead of "The cat jumped up on the chair." Teenagers with Down's syndrome may speak like two-year-olds. Working with a computer, however, such teenagers quickly picked up the idea of language structure and learned to type out their ideas and feelings in complete sentences. Researchers are excited by this new technique for helping children with Down's syndrome to learn to communicate and develop to their full potential.

8 *Speaking Effectively*

Does your speech work for you or against you? Do you have the kind of voice that people could enjoy listening to all day, or does it remind them of chalk squeaking on a blackboard? Can you think on your feet, or do you come up with your best witty remarks at two in the morning when it's too late and you should be sleeping? Do people pay attention when you talk? (Are you worth listening to?) Do you really listen when other people talk? Can you present ideas clearly, logically—and interestingly? Do you say what you mean and mean what you say?

What do you want your speech to do for you? On any particular day, you may have a casual chat or a heart-to-heart talk. You may be trying to sell ads for the yearbook or to persuade someone to go to the movies with you. You may need to find out some information by making telephone calls. You may have to give a speech to a group.

Obviously, no one set of general rules or instructions could cover all these situations, as well as talking to your cat and arguing with your sister. But there are some guidelines that are generally useful and others that can be helpful on particular kinds of speaking occasions.

First of all, take care of your equipment. That seems like an obvious bit of advice if you want to be sure of reliable, trouble-free operation of a typewriter, a baseball glove, or an electric stove. But you tend to use your voice without thinking much about the process, not taking any precautions to keep it from going out of order. In her book, *Speak to Win*, speech professor Georgiana Peacher suggests six simple rules for keeping your voice healthy:

1. Keep your head straight when you talk. If you slouch or bend your head over when you are reading aloud or talking on the telephone, you will put pressure on your larynx and interfere with proper breathing.

2. Breathe from the abdomen and don't wear tight clothes that restrict the breathing movements of the body or larynx.

3. Try to avoid clearing your throat or coughing (swallow, pause, or take a deep breath instead) or do it as gently as possible.

4. Try to keep your mouth closed when you are out in cold or damp weather.

5. Don't talk much when you're overtired, hungry, thirsty, or under a severe emotional strain.

6. If you have to talk above a constant noise, such as

in the subway, in a factory, or on a crowded street, try to rest your voice frequently. Yawning, rotating the head, shaking the head with the jaw open loosely, and breathing deeply in and out can help to relax strained larynx muscles.

The sound of your voice and your manner of speaking have a great influence on how people react to you— whether they find you likable, interesting, and worthy of respect or irritating, boring, and contemptible. Have someone record your speech on a tape recorder when you are not aware of it, and then listen to yourself. Listen critically, as though it were the voice of a stranger you were meeting for the first time. Does your voice sound too high, strained, or whining? That may be a nervous habit you have developed and can correct with a conscious effort. Do you vary your tones, or do you speak in a dull monotone? Are your intonations appropriate to the meaning of your words? Can you hear emotion in your voice? What about pace? Do you talk so quickly that your words run together and are hard to understand? Do you talk so slowly that people fall asleep listening to you? Do you articulate clearly? Do you sound like someone you'd enjoy having for a friend?

If you have noticed some deficiencies in your voice and would like to work on improving your speech, you can find books with helpful suggestions and exercises in your local library or bookstore. (Some of them are listed in the section at the end of this book, "For Further Reading.")

Most speaking takes place in conversations.

Most of your speaking probably takes place in conversation with one or more people. Some conversations are strictly for pleasure. You can't plan a good social conversation in advance. It begins spontaneously and meanders along, skipping from one topic of interest to another. Along the way, there may be touches of humor, a sharing of information and insights, and perhaps the forging of an emotional bond. You can help make conversations enjoyable by really listening actively while another person is speaking, rather than just giving the impression of polite attention while you are busily planning what you will say the next time it is your turn to speak. And don't interrupt, or finish other people's sentences for them. Asking questions—open-ended questions that encourage others to talk about their background, interests, or feelings—can help to keep a conversation moving along. But don't pry or ask intimate personal questions if the other person seems uncomfortable. What you say will be more interesting if you don't clutter your speech with meaningless words and phrases like "you know," "I mean," or "uh." Bragging, name dropping, using words that most people don't know or understand, and repeating old stories or jokes that you know the others have already heard are good ways to kill a conversation and make yourself unpopular.

What about gossiping? Gossip has a bad reputation, but it can serve some good purposes. Exchanging confidences helps to forge a bond between people and can build and strengthen friendships. Gossip can help to keep people informed about the world. It can provide a way to explore moral issues or to discuss important topics that are too sensitive to talk about directly. It can even work as therapy, helping people to vent their tensions, anxieties, and resentments. But avoid malicious gossip—it might hurt the people you are talking about, and it may eventually come back to bite you if they find out what you said. One thing to remember in gossiping: Don't talk about confidential matters if you really don't want them to be repeated.

Serious conversations generally have a specific purpose or subject. They are most effective if you pick the right time and place—circumstances that allow you plenty of time to explore the subject without distractions or interruptions. Try to keep an open mind as different viewpoints are exchanged, and don't try to argue with people about matters of taste, faith, or strong beliefs. You won't succeed in changing their minds, no matter how strong your arguments may seem, and you may wind up as enemies. Ask questions as clearly as possible, listen carefully to the answers, and try to digest and comment on them before you go on to another question. Stick to the issues, and don't get sidetracked onto irrelevant matters.

Educator and philosopher Mortimer J. Adler notes that a good conversation, like a play or a symphony, has a beginning, a middle, and an end. The beginning should focus on the *theme*, the problem or subject to be discussed. The middle should be a lengthy exploration of the subject, bringing out differences of opinion and arguments in support of them. The end should bring the conversation to a conclusion—with an agreement or decision or simply an acknowledgment that no agreement has been reached and the subject needs to be discussed further at some later time.

Educator Alan Garner suggests a simple technique for defusing tense situations, handling criticism constructively, and resisting manipulation gracefully. He advises starting out the response by *agreeing with the truth*—either the elements of truth in what the other person says or merely his or her right to an opinion. ("I can see how you would feel that way.") Then you can proceed to your reasons for your own actions or opinions without eliciting an automatic negative reaction. If you feel that a criticism is valid and intend to change, saying so will generate good feelings. But don't give a lip-service promise to change if you have no intention of doing so—that will just set up another criticism later. Acknowledging the problems your behavior may create for others is a more honest approach and gives the other person the feeling that you have at least considered and valued the suggestions. If you don't want to do something that someone else is requesting with a whole series of persuasive arguments, Garner suggests a combination of agreeing with the truth and another technique: the *broken record*, repeating your intention or opinion, with minor variations, until the other person gives up trying to manipulate you.

At various times, you may be called upon to speak on some subject before a group of people. When that happens, you may find yourself agreeing with the anonymous wit who said, "The brain starts working the moment you are born and never stops until you stand up to speak in public." There are ways to get around this sort of mind-freeze, however.

The first rule for successful speech making is to be prepared. Research the topic so that you know it thoroughly, and organize the points you want to present into a logical sequence, tailored to fit into an appropriate amount of time. While you are researching and thinking about your subject, be alert for striking facts or pertinent anecdotes that might be used as a catchy, attention-getting opening for the speech. Once you have captured the attention of your audience, they will be more receptive to the ideas or arguments you want to present.

You may write out your speech completely, as though it were an essay; or your notes may consist of just an outline, a framework of topics to be treated with some key phrases to jog your memory and guide your thoughts. Reading from a completely written speech is often deadly dull, but a brief outline may not be enough to enable you to remember all the facts and ideas you wanted to cover or to phrase them clearly and effectively. Mortimer Adler suggests a compromise: Write out the speech in the form of whole sentences, but in outline form, with ample spacing. That way you will be able to follow your flow of thought more readily and you will be less likely to lose your place in your notes while you are speaking.

Learning the speech so well that you can deliver it from memory (incorporating variations and changes where that seems appropriate) can be much more effective than reading a speech from notes. Actor-comedian Steve Allen suggests that if you don't have enough time to memorize a speech completely, or it is too long to remember effectively, concentrate on the beginning and the end. If you start out by delivering the introduction to your speech from memory, looking steadily at your audience without consulting your notes, you will create the impression that you know your material thoroughly. That impression will carry over through the middle portion, when you do consult your notes, and will be reinforced as you end with your memorized conclusion. The end of your speech should summarize some of the main points you have discussed or, if there is not enough time for that, repeat the major conclusions and, if appropriate, encourage your audience to take action on them.

As for that deadly brain freeze that may hit just when you are about to begin speaking, console yourself with the fact that a little stage fright is a perfectly natural human reaction. It lessens as you gain experience in public speaking, and even in your early attempts it tends to go away after you have plunged into the actual speech. Try to focus not on yourself and your feelings but on the subject you will be talking about.

Being prepared for giving a speech means not only researching and writing it, but also rehearsing it a number of times beforehand. Reading the speech out loud helps you become familiar with the material, determine how long it is running and whether some parts need to be expanded or shortened, and practice phrasing, emphasis, and other aspects of your delivery. You may find that some sentences come out sounding too stiff or formal, or too complicated to follow, and those can be changed as needed. Remember that although the draft of the speech was written down, the final version is meant to be *spoken*, not read, and spoken language is simpler than written language, both in vocabulary and in grammatical construction.

When you deliver your speech, clear articulation is important, but try to keep your pace and phrasing as natural as possible. Don't let nervousness make you race through the words; nor should you slow down so unnaturally that you sound pompous or boring.

Good speakers are sensitive to their audiences. An alert, listening silence can be an encouragement that the message is getting across. A ragged chorus of coughing, foot shuffling, and low-level conversation, on the other hand, indicates that you are losing their attention. The prudent speaker knows that is a time to either insert a lively anecdote or skip a few pages of notes and bring the speech to a graceful conclusion.

9 *Speech for the Deaf*

A few hundred years ago, it was generally thought that people who were born deaf could not learn to speak. True, deaf mutes were not really mute. They could make sounds, but those sounds did not carry any meaning for the average hearing person; many deaf people were thus wrongly believed to be mentally deficient.

One of the first systematic attempts to teach deaf people to communicate occurred in Spain in the seventeenth century. According to Spanish law, only people who could speak were allowed to inherit property. So rich families with deaf sons hired tutors to try to teach them to speak. Juan Pablo Bonet devised a scheme for developing language through the use of gestures, hand signs, writing, and a *manual alphabet*, an alphabet in which the letters are represented by finger positions. Then sounds were linked with the letters, and speech was developed, using special exercises that promoted mental development.

Another famous teacher of the deaf, the Abbé Charles Michel de l'Épée, worked in France in the eighteenth century. De l'Épée was not interested in teaching the deaf to produce verbal speech; that can be a long and difficult process, requiring a great deal of individual tutoring. Instead, de l'Épée developed a method for teaching large classes of deaf children to communicate by means of a manual sign language that was nearly as versatile as spoken language. A modified form of his system is still used today in many countries of the world.

Meanwhile, Samuel Heinicke, working in Germany during the same period, concentrated on developing verbal speech. He warned that the manual alphabet and signs, though sometimes useful as a crutch, can be dangerous— deaf people who have learned to communicate manually may not try to learn how to speak in sounds. The disagreement between the followers of de l'Épée and Heinicke marked the beginning of a controversy between the "manualists" and the "oralists," a controversy that is still heated and bitter today.

One of the problems in devising systems for teaching the deaf to communicate is that there are a number of kinds of deafness and varying degrees of hearing loss. In normal hearing, sound waves in the air strike the eardrum, causing it to vibrate. The vibrations are transmitted through a series of three tiny bones, linked together in a movable arrangement. Their shapes prompted fanciful anatomists to name them the *hammer*, *anvil*, and *stirrup*. The stirrup rests against the *oval window*, a membrane

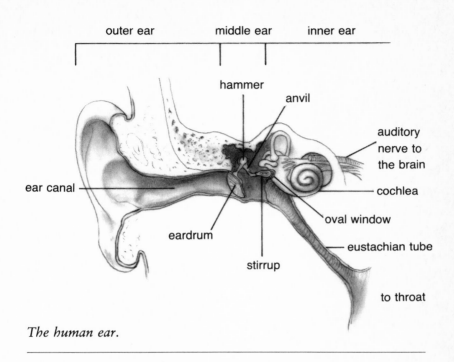

outer ear   middle ear   inner ear

hammer

anvil

auditory
nerve to
the brain

ear canal

cochlea

oval window

eardrum

eustachian tube

stirrup

to throat

The human ear.

stretched across the entrance to the inner ear chamber.
When vibrations of the eardrum set the hammer, anvil,
and stirrup jiggling, the vibrations are transmitted to the
oval window, and a wave of pressure passes into the fluid
that fills the inner ear. The vibrations travel into the
cochlea, a coiled tube shaped like a snail shell. Inside the
curving channel of the cochlea are various structures that
serve to register sounds of a whole range of frequencies
and transmit information about them to the brain. More
than twenty thousand stiff, hairlike fibers laid out cross-
wise on a membrane that runs the length of the channel

vibrate like the reeds of a harmonica, each at its own particular frequency. A structure called the *organ of Corti* rests on the membrane and contains about fifteen thousand hair cells, each with a tiny hairlike structure that sticks out into the fluid-filled channel. When a pressure wave races along the coils of the cochlea, fibers that correspond to its frequency begin to vibrate as soon as the wave reaches them. The cells of the organ of Corti riding on the membrane are jolted rhythmically in time to the vibration, and the hair cells bend back and forth. Their movement sends a message racing along a tiny threadlike nerve fiber that is one of the thousands forming the cochlear nerve. Messages from this nerve are carried to the brain, where they are sorted out; only then do we "hear."

With a complicated hearing system like that, there are plenty of places for things to go wrong. The first place is the eardrum. If it is punctured in an accident, it will not be able to vibrate. Small tears in the eardrum can heal, but large ones may remain. Infections can scar the eardrum, reducing its sensitivity. Hearing loss due to a ruptured eardrum is not complete, however, since sound can still be conducted by the ear bones.

The eardrum covers the entrance to the middle-ear cavity. An infection of the middle ear or an inflammation due to an allergy can cause fluid to accumulate, resulting in a hearing loss. The hearing loss usually clears up if the inflammation is treated successfully. Drugs can be used to shrink the membrane and dry up the excess fluids; a tiny drain may have to be inserted into the eardrum. Inflammation of the middle ear, called *otitis media*, is common among children. A middle-ear problem that often affects older people is called *otosclerosis*. Bony growths form on the tiny hammer, anvil, and stirrup and fuse them together into a single stiff mass, with the footplate of the stirrup firmly anchored to the oval window. Then the bones can no longer jiggle when the eardrum vibrates. The type of hearing loss that results is called *conduction deafness*. Sometimes it can be corrected surgically, by freeing the frozen ear bones or replacing them with an artificial part. The hearing loss in conduction deafness is relatively uniform—sounds of all frequencies become softer; so a device that amplifies sounds (a *hearing aid*) can make them louder and more distinct.

The problem is more complicated in *nerve* or *perception deafness*, where hearing loss is due to damage to structures in the cochlea, the nerves that lead to the brain, or the hearing centers in the brain itself. Sounds of some frequencies may be perceived normally while those of other frequencies are lost. (In hearing loss due to damage to the hair cells in the organ of Corti, typically the higher-frequency sounds are lost first. In our industrialized world, where our ears are constantly assaulted by noise, children can hear a much wider range of frequencies than can adults, and there is a gradual loss of hearing as we grow older.) In nerve or perception deafness, sounds are distorted. Amplifying them with a hearing aid doesn't help much; the loudness of the sounds is increased, but so is the distortion.

The audiometer measures the ability to hear sounds over a wide range of tones and loudness.

Hearing is tested with a device called an *audiometer*. Pure tones of a single frequency are presented to the person, through headphones or a loudspeaker, and the loudness is gradually increased until the tone can just be heard. That is the *threshold* for that particular tone. Hearing thresholds are determined for a series of frequencies and plotted on a graph. The resulting curve shows the amount and type of hearing loss. In another kind of hearing test, the tester reads a specially prepared list of words or sentences, and the person being tested tries to repeat them.

The average loudness of the tester's speech level is recorded on a meter, and the test is scored on the basis of whole items right or wrong or on the basis of individual speech sounds.

Oral approaches to teaching deaf children to communicate emphasize learning to read lips and to form normal speech sounds. Depending on the degree of hearing loss, this can be a very difficult task. The deaf child has to master a complicated set of fine distinctions with a spotty and inadequate set of cues. The auditory feedback that permits children with normal hearing to monitor and gradually correct their own early speech efforts is not available to the deaf child, who must laboriously observe and mimic the positions of tongue, teeth, and lips. Many deaf children have trouble learning to lip-read. They learn slowly and tend to be behind in their schoolwork, even if they are very bright. After years of practice, lipreading is still a guessing game, and some key words may be missed. Picture this scene, for example: A husband comes home from work and asks, "Where is the baby?" His deaf wife, reading his lips, thinks he said, "Where is the paper?" (*B*'s and *p*'s look alike when they are formed by the lips.) "I threw it in the wastebasket," the wife answers.

Varieties of *cued speech* have been invented to take the guesswork out of lipreading and to teach deaf children to speak. The speaker uses hand signals to distinguish between look-alike sounds like *b, p,* and *m.* Deaf children taught with cued speech quickly learn to use language and soon are reading and writing, too.

Cued speech: hand signs distinguish between consonants that may be confused in lipreading—here, between b and p.

The manual approaches to teaching the deaf, on the other hand, are based completely on hand signals. Many deaf people believe that this is a much more natural way of communicating in the silent world of the deaf and a better approach to opening a deaf child's mind to language. Studies of brain function indicate that manual sign languages are processed in the same speech areas in the dominant hemisphere of the brain as are spoken languages. People who speak with their hands are just using different senses to feed language information into the brain (vision and touch instead of hearing) and channeling the output of the speech areas into the hands instead of the mouth and throat.

One way of talking with the hands uses *finger spelling*. There is a hand position for each letter of the alphabet. Words are spelled out, using these hand gestures. Spelling out every word, letter by letter, may seem like a very long and cumbersome way of communicating, but it does work. Anyone who has seen the movie *The Miracle Worker* will remember the thrilling scene when the young Helen Keller finally understood the word *water* spelled out on her palm. (Helen's teacher had to use a specially modified version of the manual alphabet, relying only on touch, because Helen was both deaf and blind.)

Howard Hofsteater, who became totally deaf soon after he was born, writes eloquently about his deaf parents' efforts to teach him to communicate in as natural a way as possible. They decided to "talk" to young Howard constantly with their fingers, just as hearing people speak

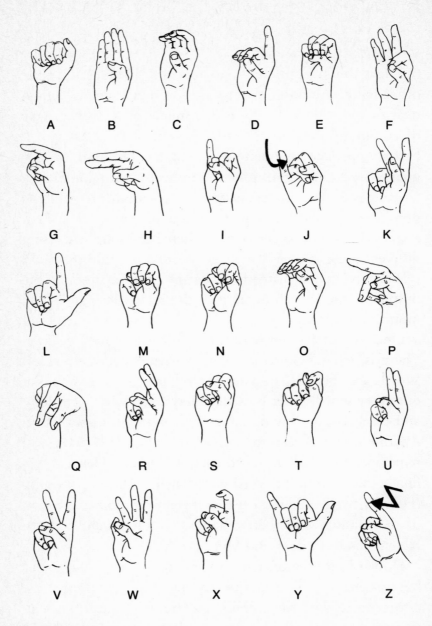

Finger spelling.

to their babies. When they changed his diaper or fed him, they continued to finger-talk, pausing now and then to emphasize a key word. For example, they would say, "Here is your milk" and then spell, "*m, i, l, k.*" They also used only finger speech when they talked to each other in Howard's presence. Their technique worked beautifully. While still in his crib, the deaf baby began to use words, spelling them out in a sort of lisping baby talk on his fingers. He would reach for his bottle and spell "*m, k.*" Other early additions to his baby vocabulary were "*w, t*" for *water*, "*p, d*" for *puddy* (custard pudding), "*pa*," "*ma*," "*c, t*" for *cat*, and "*b, n*" for *banana*. Howard Hofsteater points out that in the manual alphabet, consonants are much more distinctly formed than are vowels, and thus it was natural for him to omit the vowels in his first baby words. Gradually he learned the correct spellings—by imitating his parents spontaneously rather than being formally taught. When he was about four and a half, they taught him the written alphabet and showed him how the letters corresponded to the ones he had formed on his fingers; soon he was able to read along in the bedtime storybooks his parents spelled to him.

Howard Hofsteater was born in 1909. Today, most deaf children are taught a different kind of manual language, one that uses gestures for whole words. The American sign language developed for the deaf is often abbreviated as Ameslan or ASL. The idea of having to learn a different gesture for every word may sound impossibly difficult at first. But many of the signs in Ameslan are "natural" signs, easily understood and easy to learn. For example, you say "I love you" in sign language by holding yourself with both arms wrapped tightly in front of you.

Ameslan is a real language, with its own vocabulary and grammar—which may differ considerably from those of the spoken language. The word order is also sometimes different, and sign language omits some words that are needed in English while including signs for which there are no spoken equivalents. Ameslan has no articles and no tenses. Time is indicated by the position of the hands (the future is in front of the shoulders, the past behind them) or by modifiers such as *finish*, *up till now*, *later*, *not yet*, or *long time ago*. Information in Ameslan is always presented in the order that events happened. A typical signed sentence might be translated word for word: "Yesterday, I go party drink much eat much."

Ameslan is a flexible language. It has puns and visual rhymes, and it is "spoken" with racial and regional dialects. Its vocabulary is constantly expanding, with new signs added to represent new concepts. It can convey sophisticated thoughts and abstractions (at Gallaudet, a liberal-arts college for the deaf, courses such as sociolinguistics are taught in Ameslan), and it is wonderful for conveying emotions and telling stories. It also can be signed faster than words can be spoken. But the differences from English make it difficult for children who grow up speaking Ameslan to write standard English sentences—they tend to leave out articles, mix up prepositions, and confuse tenses. Their reading skills also tend to lag behind.

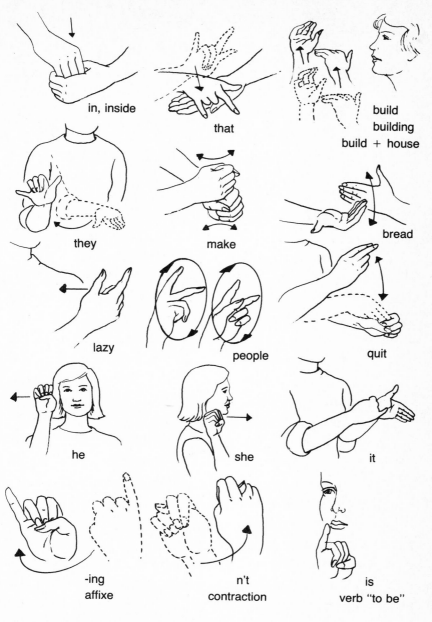

in, inside

that

build
building
build + house

they

make

bread

lazy

people

quit

he

she

it

-ing
affixe

n't
contraction

is
verb "to be"

American sign language (or Ameslan, ASL).

To remedy these problems, various attempts have been made to create sign languages more similar to standard English. But Ameslan remains popular. It is the fourth-most-used language in the United States today (behind English, Spanish, and Italian), and colleges have begun to offer programs in Ameslan or to accept a fluency in Ameslan as satisfying the foreign-language requirements for graduation. Children raised in Ameslan-speaking homes begin signing naturally, usually before they are a year old. They learn the manual language quickly, and their vocabularies are just as large as those of normal-hearing children who learn spoken speech. Children with normal hearing who are raised by deaf parents typically grow up bilingual, signing and speaking in a natural manner. They may have to act as interpreters between their parents and the hearing community, an experience that can be both stressful and rewarding. Some go on to use their bilingual abilities in careers, teaching the deaf or acting as interpreters in such varied surroundings as courtrooms (permitting deaf people to serve on juries without missing any key testimony) and airplanes in flight (a bilingual flight attendant can relay the captain's messages and help deaf passengers to feel comfortable).

Many deaf people believe that signing is the best way to teach deaf children. But there is a drawback. People who know only Ameslan and cannot lip-read are unable to communicate with most hearing people. They tend to stay in a tight little community of the deaf, where they can be understood and feel comfortable. Signing is so easy that deaf children who have learned Ameslan may not cooperate with teachers who try to teach them to lip-read. Later, when they must go out into the hearing world and work for a living, they are at a great disadvantage.

Children of a Lesser God, an award-winning play that was made into a hit movie in 1986, dramatizes some of the problems of speech for the deaf through the love story of a hearing man and a deaf woman who refuses to learn verbal speech. The success of the movie was a landmark achievement for the handicapped because Marlee Matlin, the Oscar-winning actress who played the leading role, is deaf. People around the world, watching the Oscar presentations on television, saw her give her acceptance speech in sign language.

10 *Are We Alone?*

In Baytown, Texas, a few years ago, the police had some crime-solving help from an unusual witness. Baby was alone in the house when the burglary occurred, and at first she just sat and listened while the thieves searched for valuables. Suddenly she spoke out of the darkness, and the startled burglars fled. Later the owner of the house came home, and Baby talked excitedly. "Come here, Robert," she said. "Come here, Ronnie." The owner didn't know anyone named Robert or Ronnie, and she told the police about Baby's words. Sure enough, the police investigation turned up suspects named Robert and Ronnie, along with another accomplice. The men were linked to a series of house burglaries involving the loss of $50,000 in property through the testimony of a talking bird! Baby was a yellow-headed Amazon, who had learned the intruders' names as she listened to them talking to each other.

Birds, like humans, are capable of producing a great variety of sounds. Some species, including crows, starlings, mynas, and parrots, can mimic human speech, producing words or whole sentences that are readily understandable. Is this speech? Not really. The birds can learn and reproduce patterns of sounds that form spoken words, but there is no firm evidence to indicate that they have any understanding of the meaning of the words. The stories about the parrot who seems to carry on conversations with its owner or the old myna who invariably runs through its repertoire of curse words whenever its owner's prudish aunt comes to visit make good anecdotes, but they can be explained as coincidences. (The many times the birds come out with inappropriate remarks don't make good stories and thus don't get told.)

Birds do use sounds to communicate, but they generally produce them in the form of a set repertoire of songs. A bird sings to announce that he is there, ready to defend a territory or perhaps to seek a mate. Bird sounds can also serve as signals among members of a flock or between parents and their young, as announcements of food, or as warnings of danger. Songs are learned by listening to other birds sing, but there also seems to be a built-in ability for singing a song of a particular type. Birds that are raised in isolation and never exposed to the songs of other birds produce a rather simple song that is a crude but recognizable version of the song typical of their species. There is a period when birds are particularly sensitive to picking up the song patterns of their species: usually when the bird is close to a year old, approaching its first breeding season. But the process of learning new song variations from others and introducing improvements of its own may go on throughout the bird's life. Birds of some species, such as the brown thrasher, may build up a repertoire of more than two thousand songs.

Some birds can learn only the songs of their own species. If they are exposed to the songs of other kinds of birds, even during the sensitive period, they make no attempt to copy them. There seems to be a sort of built-in mental filter to keep their song characteristic of their own kind. There are individual differences, however; and birds of the same species but from different localities may exhibit local "dialects." These regional differences in song help birds to distinguish residents of the neighborhood from strangers who may be trying to move in from another locality.

The mental filter seems to be lacking in some bird species whose members are natural mimics. Mockingbirds, starlings, wrens, and sparrows imitate the songs of many different kinds of birds that they hear. Some kinds of birds mimic other sounds from their environment. Thrashers, for example, can imitate not only other birds, but also the croaking of frogs, the chirping of crickets, and the cries of mammals. A crow may imitate the squawk of a hen, the whine of a dog, or human laughter. The bowerbirds of New Guinea and Australia have been heard imitating automobile horns, the sound of falling gravel, and the "thunk" of woodcutters chopping down trees. The birds that are skilled mimics often imitate the songs of more aggressive species. Mockingbirds, for instance, imi-

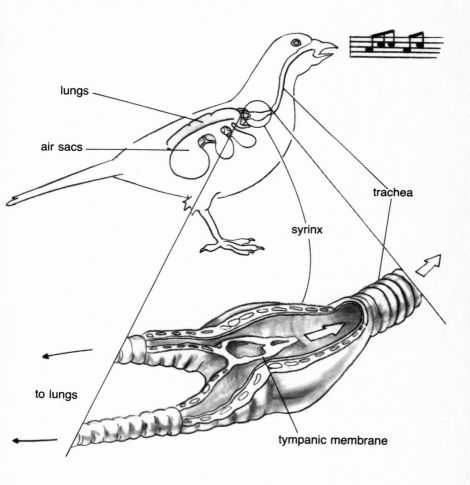

lungs

air sacs

trachea

syrinx

to lungs

tympanic membrane

Birdsong is produced in the syrinx, a sound-producing organ that can generate two different notes at the same time.

tate the calls of blue jays, which aggressively attack the nests of many songbirds. In that way, the mockingbirds can frighten away potential rivals by convincing them that there are dangerous blue jays in the neighborhood, thus protecting their own nests and food supply.

The bird's sound-producing organ is called the *syrinx,* a resonating chamber with a series of vibrating membranes located at the fork of the windpipe at the bottom of the trachea. Air from the lungs is forced through the syrinx and passes up the long tube of the trachea to the bird's mouth. The membranes divide the syrinx into two channels, and birds are actually capable of producing two different, unrelated notes at the same time, one from each side of the vocal apparatus. Although birds cannot articulate the way humans do, using tongue, teeth, and lips, the movements of the bird's head as it sings can act to modify the vocal tract, varying the length of the trachea, constricting the syrinx, or flaring the throat or beak, and thus adding to the variety of sounds.

Researchers have discovered that bird song is controlled by specialized control areas in the left hemisphere of the brain, just as speech is controlled by the left hemisphere in most humans. If a bird's left brain is damaged, however, the right side can learn fairly readily to take over the song functions. In most bird species, the male does most of the singing, and the cerebral cortex in a male bird is generally better developed than that in a female. This crucial area of the brain is also better developed in birds with a large song repertoire, and it expands in size just before the mating and breeding season, when a lot of singing will be necessary. A large area of the bird's brain is devoted to processing sound information. Some complex bird songs include as many as eighty separate notes per second. To humans, such sounds seem to be one continuous note, but birds can distinguish among them and respond to them with amazing speed. A mating pair may sing a duet, taking turns in producing the complex melody and switching back and forth so quickly that humans have to film and tape-record the action and slow it down to figure out which bird is singing which part. An intruder may engage in a song duel with the bird defending the territory. As the two sing at each other, one may switch to another song in his repertoire, and the other quickly follows, changing to a similar song type. Birds' auditory responses are as much as ten times as fast as those of humans.

Birds' songs fall into the range of human hearing, and we enjoy listening to them. But to find real speech, we have had to look to other species.

It might seem unlikely that one of the best candidates for a speaking animal is a sea mammal, the dolphin. In some ways, this species seems very alien to us, with our land-based life, our strong reliance on our sense of sight, and the many uses of our manipulating hands. Dolphins are streamlined for life in the sea, with their sleek, fish-shaped bodies and tough rubbery hides that minimize turbulence and resistance to movement through the water. Dolphins may look superficially like fish, but they are far smarter than any fish. Some scientists believe that they may be the most intelligent animals on our planet, next to humans. The *cerebrum,* the thinking part of the brain, is just as large and prominent in a dolphin as it is in a human; like our brain, the dolphin's brain has numerous surface folds and grooves, or *convolutions,* that greatly increase its surface area and thus its capacity for storing and processing information. (In fact, the brain of a bottle-nosed dolphin has a surface area twice that of a human brain.)

Even though they look like fish, dolphins are mammals and must come to the surface of the water periodically to breathe. They breathe through a single large nostril, or *blowhole,* at the top of the head. The blowhole, shaped like a crescent moon, closes when the dolphin dives and

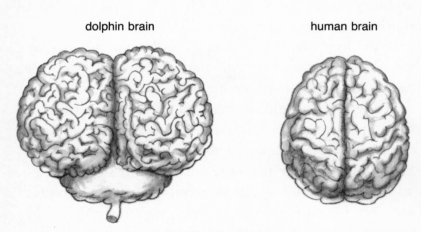

dolphin brain   human brain

The dolphin's brain actually has more information-storage capacity than the human brain.

opens when it comes up to breathe. The blowhole can produce a rasping or clicking noise, and in addition, the dolphin's larynx, located below the blowhole, can generate other sounds: squeaks, whistles, and barks.

Sounds carry well through water, and sound plays an important role in the dolphin's life. First of all, it finds its prey, avoids obstacles, and navigates with the aid of a sort of sonar system. The dolphin sends out waves of high-pitched sound—some too high-pitched for human ears to hear—and then receives and interprets the echoes produced when the sounds bounce off objects. The sound-analyzing area of a dolphin's brain is highly developed—comparable to the large area of the human brain devoted to the analysis of visual images. Dolphin sonar is so efficient that they can locate their prey in water too dark or murky to see through.

In addition to their sonar, dolphins use sounds to communicate with others of their species. Dolphins are sociable animals and usually live in schools of up to a hundred or more. Marine researchers have listened in on dolphin conversations and tape-recorded them. They have heard definite exchanges of sounds, with one dolphin "speaking" and then pausing to listen while another takes its turn.

In the 1950s, neurophysiologist John C. Lilly conducted a series of studies of dolphins, mapping their brains by stimulating different areas with electrodes. In the course of his studies, Lilly noticed that dolphins sometimes mimic sounds that they hear, such as a burst of laughter. Replaying tape recordings of some of the research sessions, Lilly and his associates discovered that their dolphin subjects were actually repeating words and phrases that the scientists had used, in a high-pitched, compressed manner so that each dolphin utterance lasted only a second or two. That unexpected discovery led to further studies, and in 1961 Lilly published a book, *Man and Dolphin,* that began with the sentence "Eventually it may be possible for humans to speak with other species." The book sparked a wave of interest in dolphins, and studies of their intelligence and speech capacity have continued.

Current studies use computers to translate human speech into high-pitched whistles and clicks that can be more readily heard and reproduced by dolphins. The sound patterns the dolphins produce in imitating the sounds are analyzed by computer and matched to the computer-generated patterns. Researchers are trying to establish a common third language that would permit humans and dolphins to communicate freely.

Are the dolphins just "parroting" words, mimicking sounds and learning patterns by rote without understanding their meanings? There is some evidence that this is not what is happening. Dolphins have not only learned to respond to spoken commands, performing complicated sequences of tasks at human request, but they have also shown an ability to grasp the meaning of unfamiliar commands by putting together the sense of the words that compose them. For example, dolphins can respond to a sentence like "Touch gate Frisbee" (meaning "Touch the gate with the Frisbee") when they have never heard that particular sentence before, although they have learned the individual words in other combinations.

While some researchers have pinned their hopes on dolphins as the most likely "speaking" animals, others have been working with some of our closer relatives—chimpanzees, gorillas, and orangutans. These apes are far more intelligent than dogs, cats, or any other animals—with the possible exception of dolphins and their relatives. Various tests have shown that they can reason in an amazingly "human" way. Chimpanzees, in particular, have been observed using tools both in the laboratory and in the wild. In one series of experiments, chimpanzees were able to get a banana dangling out of reach by dragging over a chair to climb up on, picking up a stick to knock it down, or—if one stick was not long enough—fitting two sticks together. Naturalist Jane Goodall has observed wild chimpanzees carefully selecting and shaping grass stems and twigs into tools to fish termites out of their mounds.

There have been a number of attempts to teach chimpanzees to speak. In 1947, Keith and Cathy Hayes began a long-term project of raising a young chimpanzee named Viki in their own home, treating her like a human child. Viki eventually learned to produce four intelligible words, *Mama, Papa, cup,* and *up,* as well as a few other verbal symbols of her own invention. (She clicked her teeth to ask to go out in the car and said "tsk" when she wanted a cigarette.) Viki's vocabulary bogged down at that point, even though she was eager to communicate with her foster parents, because of some limitations inherent in her species. The ape vocal tract simply is not designed for fluent speech. Although a chimpanzee has vocal cords very much like those in the human larynx, its larynx is much higher up in the neck, so that the windpipe actually makes contact with the nasal passages. There are advantages to that arrangement: An ape can breathe through its nose while simultaneously drinking a liquid or swallowing a bite of food, without any danger of choking. In humans, in contrast, there is a *pharynx,* a shared passageway that leads both to the food pipe *(esophagus)* and to the windpipe *(trachea).* When we eat or drink, a flap of tissue called the *epiglottis* comes down like a trapdoor and closes off the entrance to the trachea so that the food or liquid will not enter the breathing passages. Sometimes the epiglottis does not work fast enough and we "swallow something down the wrong pipe," then cough and sputter until it is out. An ape doesn't have that problem, but it also does not have the versatile resonating chamber that our vocal tract possesses. It is no coincidence that most of Viki's words did not require much voice resonance.

The failures of the early experiments in ape speech, such as that of the Hayeses, did not mean an end to the efforts to teach apes to communicate with humans. Instead, researchers shifted to languages that might be better suited to the apes' natural abilities—languages based on the use of the hands.

In 1969 another researcher couple, R. Allen Gardner

and his wife, Beatrice T. Gardner, began Project Washoe at the University of Nevada. Washoe was an eight-month-old chimpanzee. Like the Hayeses, the Gardners took a young chimp into their home to raise like a human child. They made no attempt to teach Washoe verbal speech, however; instead, they taught her Ameslan. Within a few years, Washoe had acquired an active vocabulary of 132 Ameslan signs, and she could recognize many more. She not only learned the hand signs for many words, but she could also put them together into sentences. "Give me tickle" was one of the combinations she invented. (She loved to be tickled.) Washoe also used her signs in creative combinations for naming things for which she had not been taught any signs. She called the refrigerator the "open food drink," and when she saw a swan for the first time, she signed, "water bird." Like Viki (who once sorted a photograph of herself into a pile of pictures of humans, right on top of a photo of Eleanor Roosevelt, while she put photos of other chimpanzees with the dogs and cats), Washoe considered herself a person. The first time she saw an adult male chimpanzee, she called him, in Ameslan, "big black bug."

Washoe did not use the signs she learned only for communicating with her human trainers. She was sometimes observed "thinking aloud." Turning the pages of a magazine one day, for example, she came to a picture of a tiger and signed *cat;* looking at a liquor advertisement, she made the sign for *drink.*

The researchers were eager to see whether Washoe would

teach sign language to her children when she was old enough to have them. Unfortunately, her first baby was stillborn, and her second died of pneumonia soon after birth. Then Washoe was given a young orphan chimp, Loulis, to raise. Loulis did, indeed, learn to sign, imitating his foster mother and other signing chimps in the group. Although the human observers purposely did not sign directly to Loulis, he quickly picked up words like *hug, drink, food, fruit, come, give me,* and *that.* After six months, he began to put signs together. The first combination he used was "drink that," pointing to the water faucet in the cage.

While Washoe was learning American Sign Language, another chimpanzee, Sarah, was being trained to communicate in a completely artificial language, devised by David Premack. Working at the University of Pennsylvania, Premack taught Sarah the meanings of plastic pieces of differing sizes and shapes, set up on a magnetic board. Each plastic symbol stood for a word or a concept (such as "the same as"), and Sarah apparently was able to use them to ask and answer questions.

Some language researchers have voiced doubts about the apes using sign language or artificial languages such as Yerkish, developed at the Yerkes Primate Center at Emory University in Atlanta. (In Yerkish, symbols generated by a typewriter hooked into a computer stand for objects, actions, and attributes and are used to write sentences.) The skeptics claim that the apes are not really communicating but just performing tricks, going through stereotyped routines that they have learned will bring re-

Washoe

Sarah

Washoe was taught American sign language, while Sarah learned to manipulate symbolic shapes.

wards. They claim that many of the apes' responses are inadvertently prompted by the trainers through unconscious gestures or body language that serve as cues; or that the interpretations of the apes' signs show more creative imagination on the part of the human observers than on the part of the apes.

Since the pioneering studies, however, a number of chimpanzees, gorillas, and orangutans have been taught the fundamentals of language, and they do something that certainly looks like conscious communication. A chimp called Lucy, for example, put Ameslan signs together appropriately to name new objects. She called a watermelon a "drink fruit," and after biting into a radish, she promptly named it a "cry hurt food." She also used sign language to express emotion. One day, as she stared forlornly out the window watching her human foster mother leaving the building, she was observed signing to herself, "Lucy cry."

Language-using apes also sign to each other. According to Roger Fouts, who has worked mainly with chimpanzees, apes usually speak to each other in incomplete sentences (as humans do when they are speaking casually), and their main topics of conversation are things like grooming, playing, and getting along together. "If the play gets rough," says Fouts, "you might actually get someone blaming someone else, someone claiming to be good." When things get really rough, the apes throw in a few curse words, like *dirty* or *rotten*.

Recently, the public's imagination has been captured

by the continuing story of Koko, a gorilla with a sign-language vocabulary of more than six hundred words. When psychologist Penny Patterson, who works with Koko and her mate, Michael, at the Gorilla Foundation south of San Francisco, asked Koko what she wanted for her twelfth birthday, Koko asked in sign language for a cat. She picked out a tailless Manx male kitten from a litter of three, named him All Ball, and cared for him tenderly until he slipped out of the cage one day and was run over by a car. Koko cried when she was told (in verbal speech) that her kitten was dead, and her fans around the world waited anxiously for reports on efforts to find a replacement. The first kitten she chose, another tailless Manx cat, turned out to prefer Koko's mate, Michael, who named the orange kitten Banana. Koko renamed the kitten Lips, and a custody dispute was averted by giving the couple another kitten, whom Koko named Smokey. Patterson hopes that the experience of caring for the kittens will help to stimulate maternal behavior when Koko has babies of her own.

At the University of Tennessee in Chattanooga, Lyn Miles has been teaching Ameslan to an orangutan named Chantek. In addition to more than a hundred signs, Chantek has picked up a rudimentary understanding of economics. For doing chores like cleaning up her room, the orangutan earns tokens that she can spend on special treats.

At the Language Research Center near Atlanta, the focus now is on pigmy chimps, a rare ape species that is believed to be genetically closest to humans. These apes are learning Yerkish, as well as an understanding of spoken language. The star pupil is a young chimp named Kanzi, who learned on his own to use keyboard symbols by watching the scientists teach his mother. At the age of four, Kanzi had developed language skills comparable to those of a one- to two-year-old human child.

The question of whether using Yerkish is really a form of communicating or just a series of clever tricks may

Kanzi

The pigmy chimp Kanzi learned to communicate in Yerkish by watching researchers teach his mother to use the keyboard.

finally be resolved in another study going on in Atlanta, at the Developmental Learning Center at Georgia Regional Hospital. In 1981, speech therapists began work with a group of fourteen severely retarded people, using Yerkish in an effort to teach them to communicate. Eight of the patients have made considerable progress, mastering dozens of symbols and becoming able for the first time to communicate their wants and needs. (The teachers began by teaching the pupils the symbol for their favorite food.) As their communication skills improve, the retarded pupils' behavior often improves as well. Several of them have been approved for placement with families or in group homes, and a pilot project is extending the Yerkish program to retarded students in the local public schools. The researchers hope that a lightweight, economical version of their Yerkish keyboard will be developed to help people with communication problems in homes and schools. "Ten years from now," says psychologist Duane Rumbaugh, who invented the language, "I hope this looks like a very primitive beginning."

11 *Talking Machines*

While language specialists continue to argue about whether we humans are the only living species capable of true speech, our world is being invaded by another type of talking creature—talking machines.

In hundreds of supermarkets across the United States, talking cash registers announce the price of each item, the total, and the change due the customer. Elevators in new buildings call out the floor and warn passengers to "please stand clear of the doors" or "please put out your cigarette." Talking dashboards in cars nag us to buckle our seat belts and warn us when the gas is getting low. Talking Coke machines greet customers, ask them to "make your selection, please," and remind them "don't forget your change." Blind shop owners can place a bill under a sensor, and a synthesized voice will inform them what denomination it is. Blind students can go to the library and use a machine that will read a whole book to them. Even dolls and stuffed toy animals can talk back to their young owners.

Some of the talking machines contain cassettes and play back prerecorded messages. But a growing number actually build up or synthesize spoken words from strings of phonemes, much as we humans do. The speech is generated from codes in a tiny silicon-wafer "brain" called a *microprocessor*. The simplest *speech synthesizer,* such as that in a Paper Money Identifier, has a small, fixed, built-in vocabulary. More sophisticated devices can generate practically any word in the language. The voice quality ranges from a flat, robotlike speech without intonation to highly inflected, realistically human-sounding male or female voices. (The more natural-sounding speech synthesizers are generally more expensive.)

People who are unable to speak can use an artificial voice produced by a hand-held keyboard with keys representing the various phonemes. Other versions produce speech from words typed out on a normal typewriter keyboard. FM-radio disc jockeys in Pittsburgh used this kind of text-to-speech machine a few years ago as the announcer for an entire radio show. Few of the listeners realized that it wasn't a human talking because the machine, nicknamed "Hal," gave the news, sports, and weather, told some jokes, did the lead-ins for the records, and ended the program with the line "E.T., phone home." Each sentence spoken by the machine had been typed by the disc jockeys into a computer programmed to convert the letter combinations to phonemes, which were then strung together to form realistic-sounding words and sentences.

The Kurzweil Reading Machine scans pages of printed

text and translates the words into machine-synthesized speech. The machine can be set to spell out words a letter at a time, pronounce a full word, or read complete sentences, paragraphs, or pages. Other reading machines have a variable speech rate, which can be useful for a blind person "reading" by ear. The speech rate can be speeded up for passages that need only be skimmed, then slowed down to aid understanding in difficult or important sections.

As for the talking toys, the latest models are far in advance of Chatty Cathy and other toys that said a few phrases when children of the last generation pulled the activating string. Teddy Ruxpin, a recent best-seller, has built-in computer-coded cassette tapes that move his eyes and mouth in sync with spoken stories and songs. Newer talking toys have microchip "brains" that synthesize an extensive vocabulary of words and phrases. Built-in sensors provide for appropriate responses when the toys are scratched, hugged, or tickled.

Human speech is more than just the ability to make sounds that are grouped into recognizable words. Speech also involves *listening*—hearing, recognizing, and understanding the sounds of spoken language. Computer scientists are developing machines that recognize speech, too. This is a more difficult task than might be expected in view of the ease with which human children master it. The first computerized *speech-recognition* systems had to be specially reprogrammed for each individual speaker, since each person has a characteristic style of pronouncing words as well as different voice tones and intonations. In a voice-recognition system, a spoken word is transformed into a varying electric current that forms a pattern with characteristic peaks and troughs. This pattern is then converted into a *template,* a pattern of zeros and ones that a computer can store in its memory. After the system has been programmed, the operator speaks a command and the computer searches its memory to find the template that matches the incoming pattern. The process is something like sorting through the keys on a key ring to find two that match by lining up the sawtooth patterns.

Voice-recognition devices that work on a template-matching system usually have a very limited vocabulary—often a hundred words or less. Each word must be pronounced separately and distinctly. The templates would not match if another person said the same words, and the computer would also make errors if the original operator had a cold or was tired or rushed and slurred the words. "Did you," for example, may sound more like "didja" in normal speech. A computer programmed to recognize the individual words would be unable to match "didja" to any template in its memory.

Massachusetts Institute of Technology researcher Victor Zue analyzed the problem of how people recognize speech sounds even when the speakers have different voice tones or regional accents. He decided to teach himself to read *spectrograms* (the computerized pictures of the electrical wave forms of speech) as though they were words.

When Zue examined many spectrograms, he noted that the patterns of a particular word said by different speakers might look quite different but still had certain points of similarity. The *s* in *stop,* for example, appears as a dark rectangular wedge no matter who is talking. By 1979, Zue had noticed and cataloged hundreds of identifying features of phonemes and had learned to read off syllables, words, and sentences from spectrograms. Then he conferred with computer speech researchers at Carnegie Mellon University in Pittsburgh. The result of their collaboration was a new method of computer speech recognition: Instead of comparing voice patterns to prerecorded templates, the computers were programmed to compare them to the universal characteristics that appear in the spectrograms of particular phonemes.

Speech-recognition systems are already finding many uses. United Airlines baggage handlers at Chicago's O'Hare Airport call out the names of airports as they load suitcases onto a conveyor belt. A computerized voice-recognition system routes each piece of luggage to a tray corresponding to the airport named.

Automakers are testing experimental cars with voice-activated door locks, starters, and windshield wipers. Test pilots are flying jets with voice-controlled equipment that responds to spoken commands like "arm the missiles." The National Security Agency eavesdrops on overseas telephone calls with computers that are programmed to pick out key words and then isolate and record any suspicious calls.

When an organ becomes available for transplant, medical coordinators can consult the completely computer-run telephone-alert system of the National Association of Transplant Coordinators. A voice-recognition system logs in information while a synthesized voice asks questions about the age and weight of the donor, blood type, and so forth; then the computer checks its memory banks for possible recipients and relays the information to the caller.

Raymond Kurzweil, the inventor of the Kurzweil Reading Machine, recently developed a computerized typewriter that can type from spoken dictation. With a memory of ten thousand words, the Kurzweil VoiceWriter can print words as fast as they are spoken. With price tags of over $20,000, both the Kurzweil Reading Machine and the VoiceWriter are within the reach only of libraries and other large organizations. But other voice-recognition systems, available at prices individuals can afford, have opened up a whole new world of opportunities to the handicapped. Voice-activated controls for wheelchairs have been developed, and quadriplegics, paralyzed from the neck down, can now use voice-activated computers to dial the telephone, operate a ham radio, and type out correspondence dictated a letter at a time.

Speech synthesizers and voice-recognition systems are now a reality, but there are still no machines that really "speak." Speech involves not only recognition of phonemes or words, but also understanding. To understand a spoken sentence, we must know not only the meanings of the individual words, but also a whole complex of assumptions and implications—things that aren't said. Researchers in the field of *artificial intelligence (AI)* cite the classic "Monkey and Bananas" problem to illustrate some of the difficulties involved.

A young monkey is standing under a banana tree. A bunch of bananas dangles above its head, too high to reach. Then an older monkey comes by. "I'm hungry," says the young monkey. "There's a stick under the old rubber tree," the older monkey replies. The older monkey understands not only the words the younger one has said, but also the problem it is trying to convey. The older monkey's answer assumes that the younger one will understand that the stick can be used to knock down some bananas.

If the young monkey said the same thing—"I'm hungry"—to one of today's robots, equipped with the latest in speech synthesizers and speech-recognition capacity, the robot might answer, "I understand." It has recognized the words and related them to their meanings in its memory bank, but it has no understanding of the deeper meaning—that the young monkey is asking for help.

The young monkey is frustrated by the robot's answer. "Can you help me get a banana?" it asks. "Yes," answers the robot. Now it has recognized the young monkey's problem, but it has taken the question so literally that its answer is not very helpful. AI researchers have a considerable way to go before their thinking machines will be able to have the same insight as a human, who would intuitively understand both the meanings of the words and their implications.

A new approach to building computers may eventually give thinking machines that kind of ability. The computers in use today work by performing sequences of operations, one after another. They work so fast that in some kinds of tasks they can outperform the human brain. But they lack our brain's flexibility. Some computer scientists are now trying a different approach, linking computer circuits together into a sort of neural network similar to the complex interconnections of the nerves in the human brain. A simple prototype of the *neural-network computer,* containing only two hundred processing elements (artificial neurons), can learn to speak on its own. It does this in much the same way as a human child, first babbling—trying out various strings of phonemes such as *ahh, nu, no, nunu, ru, unn*—and gradually figuring out that certain sequences of sounds form words, and strings of words make sentences. The only human input during this learning process is to tell the computer when it makes a mistake. In a day, such a neural-network computer can acquire the language skills of a six-year-old.

You can't really have a satisfying conversation with one of today's talking machines. If you ask the talking toy Bingo Bear his name, for example, he may reply, "Are your knees made of cheese?" But as computers grow more sophisticated—and more like human brains—the day may soon arrive when the talking robots of science-fiction movies are no longer fantasy but fact.

For Further Reading

Of General Interest

Fischler, Martin A., and Oscar Firschein: *Intelligence: The Eye, the Brain, and the Computer,* Addison Wesley, Reading, Massachusetts, 1987.

Fry, Dennis: *Homo Loquens: Man as a Talking Animal,* Cambridge University Press, New York, 1977.

Hahn, Emily: *Look Who's Talking,* Thomas Y. Crowell, New York, 1978.

Lilly, John C.: *Man and Dolphin,* Doubleday & Co., Inc., New York, 1961.

Lilly, John C.: *Lilly on Dolphins—Humans of the Sea,* Doubleday & Co., Inc., New York, 1975.

Linden, Eugene: *Apes, Men, and Language,* Saturday Review Press/E.P. Dutton, Inc., New York, 1974.

Linden, Eugene: *Silent Partners: The Legacy of the Ape Language Experiments,* Times Books, New York, 1986.

McCrum, Robert, William Cran, and Robert MacNeil: *The Story of English,* Viking Press Inc., New York, 1986.

Menyuk, Paula: *The Development of Speech,* The Bobbs-Merrill Company, Inc., Indianapolis, 1972.

Wolff, J. G.: *Language, Brain and Hearing,* Methuen & Co., Ltd., London, 1973.

For Improving Speech

Adler, Mortimer J.: *How to Speak, How to Listen,* Macmillan Publishing Co., Inc., New York, 1983.

Allen, Steve: *How to Make a Speech,* McGraw-Hill Book Company, New York, 1986.

Coleman, Ronald G., Bert A. Miller, and Robert M. Beagle: *Speech Communication: Its Nature, Substance, and Application,* Dickenson Publishing Company, Inc., Encino, Calif., 1975.

Fraser, Malcolm: *Self-Therapy for the Stutterer,* Speech Foundation of America, Memphis, Tenn.

Garner, Alan: *Conversationally Speaking,* McGraw-Hill Book Company, New York, 1980.

Osgood, Charles: *Speak Easy: One Hundred & One Ways to Think on Your Feet Without Falling on Your Face,* William Morrow & Co., Inc., New York, 1988.

Peacher, Georgiana: *Speak to Win,* Bell, New York, 1985 (reprint of 1966 edition).

Sarnoff, Dorothy: *Speech Can Change Your Life,* Doubleday & Co., Inc., New York, 1970.

On Sign Language

Bornstein, Harry, and Karen Saulnier: *Signing: Signed English: A Basic Guide,* Crown Publishers, Inc., New York, 1984.

Fant, Louie J., Jr.: *Intermediate Sign Language,* Joice Media, North Ridge, Calif., 1980.

Greene, Laura, and Eva Barish Dicker: *Sign Language: A First Book,* Franklin Watts Inc., New York, 1981.

Index

Illustrations are in *italics*.